Anna Theresa Sadlier, Alexandre de Lamothe

The Outlaw of Camargue

Anna Theresa Sadlier, Alexandre de Lamothe

The Outlaw of Camargue

ISBN/EAN: 9783337346256

Printed in Europe, USA, Canada, Australia, Japan

Cover: Foto ©Suzi / pixelio.de

More available books at **www.hansebooks.com**

A. DE LAMOTHE

THE
OUTLAW OF CAMARGUE

TRANSLATED BY

ANNA T. SADLIER

NEW YORK, CINCINNATI, CHICAGO

BENZIGER BROTHERS

PUBLISHERS OF BENZIGER'S MAGAZINE

CONTENTS.

THE OUTLAW OF CAMARGUE.

CHAPTER I.

MADAME THÉRÉSINE.

S HE was in the garden, which was separated from
the highroad by a hedge of prickly furze, gathering lilies and roses, pinks and jasmines, all pearly
with dew, and throwing them into one of those light
osier baskets which in Provence are called *canastelles*. All the while she was singing joyously in
the musical dialect of the Languedoc, and her song
was one known to all the *magnanarelles :*

> "O Magali, ma tant amado,
> Mete la teste au fenestroun :
> Escouto un pau aquesto aubado
> De tambourin e de viouloun !" *

> * "O Magali, my much-beloved,
> Show thyself at thy window,
> And hark to the tambours and viols
> That now serenade thee !"

Some one from behind the hedge replied, in a voice as fresh and joyous as her own

> " Ei plen d'estello aperamount;
> L'auro es toumbado,
> Mai lis estello paliran,
> Quand te veiran !" *

" Santa Maria! it is you, Monsieur Frederic!" cried the first singer, standing on tiptoe, the better to see the handsome young officer of the Queen's household who, in undress uniform and with a light portmanteau strapped to his saddle-girths, had drawn up his horse close to the hedge behind which the fair Provençale was gathering in her odorous harvest.

" As you see, dear Thérésine," replied the young man; adding, " Is Germaine in the garden?"

" Neither in the garden nor in the house," answered Thérésine. " Of course you were not expected to-day, and Mlle. Germaine went yesterday to Arles."

" Alone?"

" No, with your mother and the Commander."

" That is pleasant," said the young officer, evidently disappointed. " Can you tell me when they will be back ?"

---

* " The heaven above is full of stars,
The wind has fallen.
But the stars must pale
In seeing thee !"

" To-day, certainly, and most probably in an hour."

" I am tempted to go and meet them. Did they mention by what road they would come back ? "

" They mentioned nothing about it; but you know, if it is not by Saint-Gilles, or by les Saintes, or by the banks of the Valcarès, it will surely be through the fields."

" That is to say, by one of the four cardinal points," said Frederic, who, more and more annoyed, decapitated the flowering heads of the furze with the end of his whip. " And really it is fortunate there are no more, because I should be still more puzzled which to take."

" What would you? You know Mlle. Germaine, and are aware that she never goes over the same road twice if she can help it."

" *Ma foi*, it was well worth my while to kill my horses, and to ride post-haste here from Lyons, for the sake of being a day sooner and taking my people by surprise! I need not have hurried so much, and might have stopped to pay a flying visit at Lyons, to our cousins the de Blésignans. It would have saved me that journey which I have to take in a few days."

" In a few days?" cried the Provençale. " You are not off your horse yet, and you talk of departing."

" To return soon."

" If Mlle. Renée will let you."

"I do not see very clearly why she should prevent me. Ill as she is, she cannot have much need
of me, especially when she keeps herself shut up
between the four walls of her room, and has to take
tisanes."

"Perhaps she will go out more than you think,"
said Thérésine, with a malicious smile, which she concealed by bending over her basket of flowers. "I
should not be surprised if she came here to ride horseback, hunt partridges, and assist at our *ferrades*."

"*Ma foi*, I know her so little," said Frederic,
"that I have no idea whether she has these amazon
tastes or not, but I fancy she is quiet in her ways;
and from what Germaine, who was three years with
her at the convent in Avignon, told me, I think she
is too frail and delicate to find much charm in our
way of living."

Thérésine smiled again.

"And are you as great a hunter and fisher as you
used to be?" she asked.

"I am keener than ever about such amusements,"
said he; "and now that I have a six-months leave,
I dream of nothing but duck-covers, and fish-ponds,
and all the rest."

"Oh, then you have come back in good time.
The quail are passing here now in great numbers,
and I heard yesterday that bustards had been seen
on the Island of Tête-de-Miole."

"Bustards were really seen there?" cried the

young officer, his hunting instincts gaining the upper
hand. " I am delighted; they are royal game, a
hundred times better value than all the pheasants of
the parks of Versailles or Fontainebleau. To-morrow
at latest, having meantime embraced my mother, I
shall set out with your father for the Valcarès; the
weather is superb for shooting in the marshes, and
between our good Bernard and myself I hope we
shall bring back a load of game."

" My father would like nothing better than to
accompany you on this pleasure-party," said the
young woman, "for you know that a musket never
weighed much upon his shoulders, and that a bag
was never too heavy for him; but just now it will
be impossible for him to do it."

" What do you mean ? Will his legs refuse to
carry him ?"

" *Péchère !* for three weeks he has walked on
crutches, and now his rheumatism keeps him confined to his chair."

" Poor Bernard ! he must have been imprudent in
some way—spent too many nights *à l'espère.*"

" He is no longer young," said Thérésine, sadly
shaking her head.

" Bah! he is scarcely sixty," said Frederic. " We
shall have many a good day's sport together yet.
Unfortunately I do not know whom I shall find in the
meantime to take his place in managing the boat
and all that."

" My husband will take his place."

" Your husband?" cried Frederic in astonishment.
" You are joking.   Show me your hand."

She burst out laughing, raised her hand above the
hedge, and showed a plain band of gold upon her
finger.

" So you are really married ? "

" More than two months ago.   Did you not know ? "

" The first I heard of it ; it was a pretty trick for
you to play me, getting married without saying a
word to your foster-brother! "

" My husband begged the Commander to inform
you of our marriage, and I was sure that Mlle. Germaine had written to you about it."

" Neither of them gave me an inkling of it.   Germaine, because she is always in such a hurry to tell
the news that she often fancies she has told it in advance; and my uncle only takes up his pen to write
his rascal of a nephew a homily on the duties of
his profession."

" The nephew would much prefer a roll of louis
d'or."

" Oh, much indeed, or even a handful of pistoles,"
replied Frederic.   " But that's not the question just
now.   What is your husband's name ? "

" He is a worthy lad of your acquaintance —
Marius."

" What Marius?   There are as many of the name
here as there are quail in the Crau."

" This is Marius from the Commandery."

" There are ten at the Commandery."

" This is the one who used to hunt with you."

" Ah, Marius the huntsman, my uncle's adopted son, my rival at the chase. Yes, I know him; a worthy youth whom I used to like very much, but who did not like me."

" How can you say such a thing, Monsieur Frederic ?" cried Thérésine. " He often spoke of you, and I can assure you—"

" That he hates me because I used to have better shots than he."

" On the contrary, he likes and admires you."

" Ta! ta! ta! my Thérésine; unless he has changed, he would gladly send me to Old Nick, ever since I brought down the partridges which he had just missed; he never forgave me."

" It is true that he prides himself upon his reputation as a huntsman."

" Ha! ha! we are getting at the truth. But you see I have a double crow to pluck with you. You married without telling me a word about it, and married my enemy. However, fortunately there are the ponds and the marsh of Grand-Mar between him and me."

" We do not live at the Commandery now," said Thérésine, blushing.

" Ah, indeed! But since I find you here, your dwelling cannot be very far off," said Frederic, who, for the greater convenience of conversation, had passed his leg over the head and shoulders of his steed, and sat carelessly upon the edge of the saddle. "Where are you living now?"

"Here," smiled the Provençale. "My father is not able to do the work that he used to, looking after the timber, game, and all that. Your mother took Marius in his place."

"Better and better; in my absence you install the enemy here; there is only one thing more to be done."

"What is that?"

"Put us out, and take our places."

"Monsieur Frederic," said the young woman, her eyes full of tears, "I know very well that you are jesting; but do not say that either to my father or Marius: my husband would leave the house at once."

"Come, come, you little goose," said Frederic, "you are turning jest into earnest. Dry your eyes with that rose, and go on with your song. You Provençale women are as giddy as grasshoppers, and should be always singing like them."

"You see, it is—"

"I see you are my sister, that your husband is a good friend of mine, that we will have some fine sport together, and that, as I am somewhat rusty after these months among the Queen's Dragoons, he will have to give me a few lessons."

"Meanwhile I have left you sitting on your horse."

said Thérésine, deeply moved, "and have never thought of opening the gate for you. It was very thoughtless of me; I will run and draw the bolt now."

"No, no, stay; it is not worth while. I will get in as I can. So you fasten the gates here, now?"

"Only the gate of the courtyard; but the other gates are too low for your horse."

"Bah!" said the officer, "my horse, as you call this sorry beast, can pass anywhere; and for myself, when I find gates too low I try this plan."

So saying, and without the slightest hesitation, he rose in his saddle and, resting his hands lightly on either side of it, sprang with one bound into the garden.

"Good heavens!" cried Thérésine, "you do not seem to have grown very rusty yet. But at all events you were near putting both feet into my basket."

Frederic laughed.

"Shall I help you to gather flowers?" he said. "I have a splendid method."

And he began to cut off their heads with his riding-whip.

"Ah, stop, Monsieur Frederic, you will spoil all!" cried the Provençale, in a supplicating tone.

"What are you going to do with all these flowers?" asked Frederic. "You have enough now to decorate the whole house."

" Do you know what day this is ? "

" *Parbleu !* it's the twenty-third of May."

" Pardon me, the twenty-fourth."

" I believe you are right, but it makes no difference."

" On the contrary, it makes a great deal."

" Why ? "

" Because the twenty-fourth is the eve of the
twenty-fifth."

" It is something like, ' a quarter of an hour before his death M. de La Palisse was still alive.' I
begin to think you are making fun of me."

" You know very well that I would not take such
a liberty, Monsieur Frederic."

" I am not so sure about that. But what connec-
tion have these flowers with the twenty-fifth of
May ? "

" Only that to-morrow morning your mother,
Mlle. Germaine, the Commander, and others set out
for les Saintes."

" Oh, I forgot! to-morrow is the Feast of the
Three Marys."

" Do they not celebrate the feast on that day in
Paris ? " asked Thérésine.

" They do not concern themselves much. either
at Paris or Versailles," said the young man, laughing,
" about our poor Marys."

" Yet they are great saints," said Thérésine, in-
dignantly.

"I do not say anything to the contrary," said Frederic, "but no one knows of them in Paris."

"Then your Paris is a country of savages and heathens," said Thérésine.

The epithet "savage" applied by the peasant of Camargue to the wits and savants of the court made Frederic laugh heartily.

"I hope you have not become like them," said Thérésine, regarding him anxiously.

"No, no, do not be afraid," said Frederic, seriously. "No, thank God, I still hold, and will always hold, I hope, to my faith, my religion, my family, my country, my dear Camargue; and I assure you my greatest desire is to come back some day to lead the same life here that my father so honorably led before."

"I wish *my* father could hear you say that," said Thérésine. "You know, Monsieur Frederic, how warmly attached he is to your family; since you have been gone he often says to us: 'It would be a great misfortune if our good master were to leave the country; a great misfortune for Camargue, a great misfortune for him likewise.'"

"Why is Bernard afraid that I would leave the country?"

"Because the nobility all leave their domains to go and live in Paris or Versailles. He says the castles are vacated one after the other, and that the court attracts nobles as a mirror attracts larks."

"Your father is right, Thérésine. Every one
rushes thither; the provinces are deserted; the lords
forget the peasants, the peasants forget their lords;
the bond which unites them one to the other is
broken by prolonged absence. And as they do not
see one another, they cease to care for one another.
To-day it is indifference, to-morrow it may be
hatred; who knows where it will end? Perhaps the
sons of those who would have died to defend their
lords will be the first to set fire to their castles."

"If the lords see all this, why do they continue
to abandon their manors?" asked the Provençale,
who had suddenly become sad and serious, while dis-
tractedly plucking to pieces the petals of a rose which
had fallen from her basket.

"Ask the moths why they come every evening to
singe their wings in the flame of the lamp. Glitter
attracts men as it does insects; and if you knew the
allurements of Paris and Versailles, if you were present at the balls, reviews, banquets, if you could see
that magnificent palace of Versailles with its foun-
tains, statues, immense gardens, marble galleries,
salons resplendent with gold, its great assemblies,
its royal receptions, brilliant equipages, bustle, animation, life, if you could hear the clink of gold upon
the gaming-tables, round which stand lords and ladies
superbly dressed—"

"I like our Camargue better," interrupted Thérésine, shaking her head.

"Perhaps you are right," said Frederic; "and frankly, now that I am away from it all, I will enjoy going with you to-morrow to the Saintes-Maries, trotting on a country mare, much better than galloping, in splendid uniform, behind the King's carriage when he takes his daily drive to Marly or Fontainebleau."

"Then you will go with us to the pilgrimage," cried the Provençale, her face brightening at the thought. "You are right; it is better to honor God and His saints than to mock at religion like the fine gentlemen of Versailles, as the good Commander often told me."

· "My uncle is not far from the truth," said the traveller. "But all this is no reason why I should waste time chattering here with you, instead of trying to get the dust off my face and clothes, while you are having my trunks sent up to my room and finding me something for breakfast."

"*Péchère!* you have not breakfasted yet, at this hour of the day? I thought you had stopped at Arles, at the Inn of the *Lapin qui Saute*." *

"Certainly it would have been the wisest thing to do; but on arriving there I found no horses in the stable, so, despite the entreaties of Master Jean, the innkeeper, I came on to Trinquetaille, where I left my horse, half dead, at the other side of the bridge,

---

* Leaping Hare.

with Guillaume le Ragot, the farmer of Little Argens, who promised to send it to me by the royal post, and who gave me the wretched mare upon which I managed to reach here, following the Grande Mont-longue.''

'' You mean the Petite,'' said Thérésine, who, with her *canastelle* of flowers on her head and one hand upon her hip, was preparing to return to the house.

'' No, I tell you it was the Grande.''

'' Then you crossed the marsh of Grand-Mar ?''

'' Of course; it was the shortest way.''

'' It is well for you that there has been no rain of late or you would not have got out of it very easily.''

'' The marsh and I are old friends,'' responded the young man, laughing, '' and it was in splendid order to-day.''

'' You might have had some rough work there; the bulls are out to-day.''

'' What do you take me for ?'' cried Frederic, laughing. '' Do you think that because I wear a dragoon's uniform I have become a coward ?''

'' I do not say that; but with a bad horse and one which probably does not belong to the country, if a bull had given you chase you might have had a good deal of trouble to escape.''

'' My ' horse,' as you persist in calling it, is an old country mare which was bred in a farmyard among the cattle; and besides, the guardians are there, mounted, armed with their spears, and taking every precaution.

Your father would laugh at the idea of my going round the marsh for the sake of prudence. Would you have done it ?''

The young woman laughed, and both entered the château, which was almost deserted just then. Whilst Thérésine set down her basket of flowers and took off the large felt hat of stiff and ungraceful form, such as was then worn by all women from Durance to Var, Frederic proceeded to his room and began his toilet.

The southern peoples all have an exaggerated form of speech, likely to produce confusion of ideas in all who have not lived among them. In Italy the merest tourist hears himself constantly addressed as '' your excellency ''; a ragged Spaniard mounted on a lame donkey is called *señor caballero ;* and in Camargue the name *château* is often given to a dilapidated farm-house which is sometimes scarcely habitable.

It is true that if these rare habitations scattered over an almost uncultivated country are less than remarkable in themselves, the words of Cardinal Maury may be well applied to them: '' I am little of myself, but much by comparison.''

Now, stone houses in an island where there is not a single quarry, but where the soil is so marshy and sandy that it contains not even a pebble, are a luxury indulged in only by rich proprietors. The other inhabitants dwell either in simple cabins, which are in themselves, comparatively speaking, a luxury,

—for wood is far from being plentiful,—or, like the herdsmen (called also " guardians "), lead an almost nomad life, sleeping under low, pointed tents of a sugar-loaf form which they carry with them from one pasture-ground to another, and which, seen from afar in the naked and level plain, look like gray ant-hills scattered over the highroads or along the banks of streams.

As for châteaux properly so called—except Al-baron, a sort of citadel built upon the banks of the Lesser Rhone, not'so much to protect navigation as to levy contributions upon vessels coming or going from Saint-Gilles in the days when that town had an importance long since obscured—the less said the better.

There were no more villages. One town alone had dared to venture within the delta, and, finding there a rock quite close to the mouth of the river, had perched itself, or rather intrenched itself, upon it, growing up around a church, which is itself a fortress, erected by the piety of the faithful over the tomb of Saint Mary to protect it from the violence and rapine of the Saracens.

The *Château Rouge* belonged to the family of de Marcoiran, and it stood in the garden which Frederic had so unceremoniously entered, a modest habitation, surrounded by the buildings necessary for the cultivation of a property composed chiefly of sandy and marshy land, rather than a sumptuous dwelling.

This habitation was situated upon the banks of the Valcarès, a stream which might be called an inland sea, for it covered more than six thousand four hundred and eighty acres. The dwelling, separated from the rustic chapel of Notre Dame d'Amour by the sanitary canal known as the Petite Montlongue, formed with its vast orchard of many varieties of fruit-trees and its little forest of pines, a sort of oasis or verdant island. This island is situated almost at the central point of the triangle of seventy-three thousand acres known as the Island of Camargue and marks the division of the two branches of the Rhone which from Arles flow into the sea.

Upon the ground-floor, excepting the side which gave upon the river, where nothing else reached the eye, the view was bounded by the green hedge of furze enclosing the garden; from the first floor the panorama was more extensive; from the second and last it was limitless. On one side, the eye, passing unobstructed over the bluish surface of the lake, perceived on the horizon the shining thread of the Mediterranean, that lay like a band of silver. On the other, passing over the narrow line of meadows or harvest-fields which bordered the canal, the view lost itself in the immense flat grayish plain dotted with reedy ponds, or with the white peaks of the tents of the guardians, or with dark and moving spots, which are the bulls wandering in herds over the half-dried marshes.

Each season this landscape, which at first sight seems dull and inanimate, changes not only its features but its color.   In the spring and autumn the waters of the canal, swollen by heavy rains, fill the inland pools and increase them into great sheets of water, upon which the north wind sets in motion, like green meadows, the various kinds of reeds and rushes which are so precious to the inhabitants.   For they use them not only as food for their cattle, but carefully gather them to form a thatch for their huts and a wicker-work for chairs.   They also manufacture from them rude but impermeable mats, under which the salt-makers shelter their store of salt.

Everything is green then in the plain, and the woolly beasts come down by hundreds into the low grounds, till the heat drives them back to the mountains, to browse in the fallow lands upon the *margal*, or ray-grass, which is the best grazing for lambs.

This is eminently the season for shooting in the marshes.   Coots, curlews, and woodcock swarm in the rose-banks, where, walking about on their long legs, are flocks of red flamingoes, which are always hard to approach, because their sentinels keep such good watch.   It is beautiful, however, to see them rise into the blue heavens, displaying their great flaming wings and describing immense circles.

Then, too, Camargue is bedecked with all her bravery of flowers and foliage; long grasses spring from the sodden earth, and plants peculiar to salt meadows, thistles with yellow or blue flowers, salt-wort with its purple branches, camomile-flowers with their glaucous color, cinquefoil shining like gold, and asters bright as silver, all enamelling the humid plain traversed by troops of snow-white horses or herds of jet-black bulls.

In summer the scene changes completely. Dried up under the fiery heat of the dog-star, which it is impossible to temper in this unsheltered plain, the marshes disappear, leaving no traces but pools of stagnant and brackish water exhaling a malarial miasma. The reeds turn yellow; the dry earth assumes a dull slate-color, upon which the salt, by the effect of a rapid evaporation, settles in great white spots, or forms that effervescence which is so fatal to all vegetation. Its snowy surface crackles under the feet and retains their imprint, or comes off leaving exposed a brilliant surface.

For several weeks there is now a sort of factitious life in this dead region; it is harvest-time, and bands of gleaners and reapers come across the Rhone, scythe in hand, to cut down the rushes or, hastening into the cultivated fields, gather thence the abundant harvest.

An endless train of wagons furrows the plain and is enshrouded in clouds of warm dust. Rushes and meadow-grass fall under the keen blade and are formed into sheaves and heaped upon the carts. But time presses, the heat grows suffocating, a malarial

vapor enshrouds the whole peninsula infested by
swarms of mosquitoes, whose sting leaves neither
man nor beast a moment's rest.

In this fiery atmosphere during the day, and in
the poisonous vapors during the night, the work goes
on, with neither rest nor intermission until the harvest
is done; then the drivers crack their whips, and the
eager multitude depart with their booty, like a miser
carrying off a treasure.

Left to its isolated and pallid population, stripped
of its rushes and its harvests, Camargue assumes a
strange aspect which is not without a certain gran-
deur. But it is no longer France, it is an almost
fantastic region, a bare level plain, gray and dusty,
encircled by the two arms of the Rhone, which embrace without fertilizing it. It seems like a bit of
Africa grown colder, bereft of its palm-trees, and
where the maestral, or northwest wind of the Mediterranean, replaces the sirocco. But it has retained
its Saharran aspect, its broad melancholy horizon,
its stunted shrubbery, its monotonous silence, its
rare oases, in the shade of which are solitary edifices,
a species of Arab blockhouse, low and whitewashed;
its mirages, which are almost as frequent as in the
desert, and which raise from the midst of this desolation magical landscapes, as vague as a dream, as
fleeting as an illusion of the senses.

All this is strange, but of a drowsy, dreamy
strangeness which does not excite the imagination.

The eye wanders over the level plain, finding no object upon which to rest. The feet of the horses, which are usually of Saracen origin, noiselessly raise a cloud of almost imperceptible dust. Sometimes in the distance a gray smoke arises from the gray earth, marking the passage of a flock of sheep. These sheep, from their color, cannot be distinguished from the plain upon which they vainly seek for nourishment.

It is hard to conceive such utter sterility; yet there is water at a very short distance down in this dry soil. The island is furrowed with a network of streams; sometimes a sunbeam brightens the surface of a pond in the vicinity of which there is not a single tree. For this water is brackish; instead of being favorable to vegetation it destroys it, and, instead of turf upon the banks, the water, in ebbing, leaves only a salty substance, the whiteness and brittleness of which betray its origin. Rain has the same effect; in Camargue it only makes salt spring up from the earth.

So that, in truth, water and salt share the empire of this sterile region, and make it, each in turn, wear their livery. To live in such a country certain special qualities are evidently necessary, for these two traits, apparently contradictory, form the basis of the native character: an indefatigable patience to triumph over the difficulties of the soil, and an indomitable courage to control the cattle, which are in an almost savage state. It would seem that the difficulty of living in so unproductive a region would soon depopulate it, but the contrary is the case.

Man is born for struggle; it makes him hardy, becomes second nature to him, and forms a bond which unites him more strongly than any other to the earth which he waters with the sweat of his brow.

Nothing in the world could tempt Thérésine to leave the banks of the Valcarès without prospect of a speedy return. There was she born; there had she grown to womanhood; and for her the desolate wildness of these marshes had a greater charm than the richest and most fertile territory upon the Rhone.

Two or three times a year she was reluctantly induced to visit Arles, the Paris of la Crau and of Camargue. The tumult of so many people, the animation of the streets, the ringing of bells, the crowded thoroughfares, wearied her; she could not breathe, there was not air enough for her, in this brilliant flower of the desert. Her eyes needed the wide-stretching horizons of her country; her lungs required its broad acres perfumed by the sea. Disdaining the admiring glances which her beauty attracted, she leaped, light as a bird, to the crupper of a Camargue pony, behind her father, joyful because she was returning to her free solitude.

Vivacious and laughing, as are all Provençales, she, like many of the women of Arles, was of that

Greek type which even at the present time remains pure and intact in that ancient colony. Tall, lithe, graceful in every movement, she had won, not so much on account of the regularity of her features, or from that dazzling whiteness of complexion which resists in so astonishing a manner the heat of the sun, as from the singular sweetness of her expression and its remarkable kindliness, the surname of "the Flower of Camargue," given her by the guardians.

Besides, being equally skilful in handling the oar or riding the most fiery horse in Camargue, she was possessed of accomplishments which, on the banks of the Valcarès, are not, as they might be in England, eccentricities, but the indispensable accompaniments to the education of a woman in a country where there are no means of locomotion other than horses or boats. Her reckless daring excited the old Commander's warmest admiration, and he often said to Bernard, the old huntsman:

" Your daughter need only learn to handle a gun and she could enlist in the regiment of her foster-brother, M. le Chevalier."

" I would rather she knew how to put a patch on my drugget coat, mend my shirt, and prepare my mess of aioli or bouilla-besse," laughed the old servant of the family to which Thérésine was admitted almost on an equality.

Only two months older than Frederic, her mother had nursed them both, and Thérésine had since

shared almost equal advantages of education with
Mlle. Germaine de Marcoiran, in whose youthful
games and walks she had always had her share.
Yet any idea that she was Germaine's equal had
never yet occurred to the peasant-girl. At that
period class distinctions were more clearly defined
than in our own days, and the friendship of the two
young girls for each other did not on Thérésine's part
exclude a proper deference for the daughter of her
feudal lord.

At the present day, when everything is measured
by the standard of money, all this is changed; on the
one hand insolence, on the other envy carried to
the verge of hatred: this is what has taken the
place of the old affability and respect.

Between Germaine and Thérésine existed, then,
an intimacy, condescending on the one hand, respectful on the other. So that the two young girls
were really friends rather than servant and mistress.

In point of fact, the one who should have borne
this latter title relegated all her authority to Thérésine. Except the family correspondence, which
Madame de Marcoiran always attended to herself
unless Germaine undertook the office of secretary,
Thérésine fulfilled all the duties of prime minister
of the interior in the *Château*, or *Mas Rouge ;* she
wore at her belt the keys of office, superintended the
kitchen, and ruled over the garden and the dairy.

Left a widow even before Germaine's birth, Madame de Marcoiran had gradually withdrawn from all share in the administration of her vast domain, entrusting the exterior to Bernard, and the interior to his wife, and after her death to Thérésine. Enfeebled in health and naturally inclined to melancholy, the châtelaine of the *Mas Rouge* devoted herself entirely to the education of her daughter Germaine, who, being probably destined to pass her life amid scenes more brilliant than those in which her childhood had sped, was necessarily to be formed in the manners and accomplishments essential to a young woman of her rank and station.

For the first twelve years the noble widow had, with the help of the Abbé Boucarut, curate of Notre Dame d'Amour and tutor to Frederic, given Germaine a sufficient knowledge of history, geography, orthography, and composition, at the same time that she instilled into her, more by example than by teachings, the principles of solid piety.

But, as time passed, the good mother felt that the task she had undertaken was beyond her, and that, for her daughter's good, she must consent to part with her, for a few years at least. Germaine was accordingly sent to Avignon, where an aunt of hers was abbess of the royal convent of St. Praxeda. Her departure from the *Mas Rouge*, in company with her mother and the Commander, was most affecting, and Germaine and Thérésine, then separated for the first time, shed many tears.

In a day or two after, Germaine found herself behind the gratings, whence she was to come out no more till her education was completed. That is to say, till she had learned to curtsey, to dance or rather walk through the grave and stately minuet, to copy, with more or less skill, some models of flowers in crayon, to play long and monotonous sonatas on the spinet, to take part in the tragedies of Racine, and to sing the languid and insipid romances then in vogue, accompanying herself on the harp. This last accomplishment seems to afford an opportunity for the display of finely shaped hands and long slender fingers, the undeniable tokens of long descent and noble blood.

Germaine cared little for all these branches of knowledge, but she knew that her mother was resolved that she should acquire them; so, after a few days of pardonable despondency, during which the poor captive felt sadly that she only saw the blue sky through bars, Germaine went to work with an ardor which, if it threatened to impair her health, at least enabled her to reach the goal before many of her companions, some of whom had to remain two or three years longer.

At sixteen Germaine's education was finished, and she left school and returned to the *Mas Rouge*, to the great joy of Thérésine, who found her much paler and thinner, but as simple and good as ever.

Frederic was no longer there. Through the in-

fluence of his uncle the Commander, the young noble
had got a commission in the Queen's Dragoons, into
which Monsieur de Thémine had admitted him out
of regard for his old friend.

At his departure the young man also felt considerable regret in leaving the scene of his hunting
exploits; but the thought of wearing a brilliant uniform and taking part in all the festivities and pleasures
of the court, and seeing Paris, of which he had heard
such enthusiastic descriptions, consoled him in great
measure for all that he left behind. He stopped at
Avignon on his way, to present his respects to his
aunt and to embrace his sister.

It was then that the latter had presented him to
Mlle. Renée de Blésignan, her companion and friend,
who, pale and sickly, did not leave any very great
impression upon his mind.

He had been absent four years, and returning now
for a six-months leave, he had to renew his acquaintance with all the inhabitants of the *Mas Rouge.*

CHAPTER II.

FATHER-IN-LAW AND SON-IN-LAW.

IN his own room, which no one had inhabited since his departure, and where, thanks to the affectionate care of his mother, sister, and Thérésine, he found everything just as he had left it, arranged with the most scrupulous care, from his double-barrelled hunting-gun—his old companion in so many excursions—to the crucifix over his bed, above which was a blessed palm, renewed every year by some pious hand, Frederic enjoyed the delightful sense of being once more at home, where everything brought back some pleasant recollection. He had only been there a few minutes, when he heard a discreet tap at the door.

"Come in," cried the young man, who was kneeling at his open trunk, from which he was taking out various articles of dress.

A Provençal with complexion tanned by the southern sun, his legs protected by long leathern gaiters, his waist encircled by a red belt, and his head by a colored handkerchief tied under a felt hat much the worse for rain and sun, entered immediately, bringing soap and towels and one of those heavy green jars which are known in the country by the name of *dourgue.*

" Good-day, Monsieur Frederic and the company," said the new-comer, using a form of speech which to most people would have appeared extraordinary, as the salutation was addressed to only one person. The Queen's Dragoon, however, was not in the least surprised, knowing well that in Provence this mode of speech is still employed; it is a salute to you and to your guardian angel. " I hope you had a good journey."

" Excellent, my dear Marius," replied Frederic, who, without rising, gave his hand to the visitor. " Well, and so you are married, my boy."

" At your service, monsieur. Shall I fill your jug with water ? "

" No, leave the jar here. I need half the Rhone to get rid of the dust that I collected between Arles and here."

" It must have been dusty; but you, who know the country so well, should have remembered that in crossing the Grand-Mar you were sure to get all the dust."

" There is not usually so much in the month of May."

" True, but this year the heat came early, and the flocks began a fortnight since to go up into the mountains."

"Coming from Paris, of course I knew nothing of all this; but what surprised me even more was the number of locusts; in some places my mare raised a swarm of them at every step."

"That is just what I told Elzias, the guardian, two or three days ago. I said that if the sun continued as hot as it has been, we should see those vermin playing the devil with the harvests."

"It would be a pity. The crops seem very fine."

"Hum! more straw than grain so far, Monsieur le Chevalier; and if the Rau * does not blow up and bring us rain to water the ears, the sacks will not be very heavy this year."

"Ah," said Frederic, laughing, "this is not the Commandery, and our grain is not like that on the banks of the Rhone, where every inundation fertilizes the earth; but such as it is, you will see that our harvest is larger than you think."

Marius made no other answer than a gesture expressive of incredulity.

"Come, come, my boy, I see you regret having left the Commandery."

"No doubt, Monsieur Frederic, I regret the Commander, to whom I owe everything, and who has always been so kind to me; but believe that I am very glad to be in your service, and if I have one desire in the world, it is that I may always remain here."

---

* West wind.

"Capital! I can well believe it," cried a rough voice at the half-open door, and on the threshold appeared old Bernard, who, hearing of his young master's arrival, had forgotten his pains to come and salute him.

"Eh, good-day, my dear Bernard!" cried Frederic, joyfully, rising hastily and throwing himself into the old man's arms.

"Always the same good, kind Monsieur Frederic," said the old man, with tears in his eyes. "I can well believe, Marius, that you would never want to leave this blessed house. Oh, how glad I am to see you again, my good, my dear monsieur! May Heaven bless you and all your excellent family!"

"Come, my brave friend, no tears! An old veteran like you, and a soldier of the king, should not be seen with wet eyes. Sit down, my poor cripple. So you really love me a little."

"A little! You may well say a little, and a good deal, and more again. You see, Marius, he is almost my son, for he is the foster-child of my poor dead Thérésine; old Bernard would let himself be chopped as fine as mince-meat for any of the family."

"Come, sit down, my good fellow. Why will you torment me by standing in front of me with your rheumatic joints? Here, take my arm-chair."

"Never mind, Monsieur Frederic; another chair will do just as well for my worn-out old carcass."

"On the contrary, the older it grows the more care it needs. So into the arm-chair, Father Bernard, or I will get angry with you."

"You must always have your own way; and it's all one to me. You look well, Monsieur Frederic; your cheeks are as red as an apple."

"*Palsambleu!* I should think so."

"Do you know, Monsieur le Chevalier, that you have grown to be a splendid man? When you left us, three years ago come Saint Matthew, you were full two inches shorter and your mustache scarcely shaded your lip. Now one would think it was marked with coal."

"Don't speak of it. I have not been able to shave for four days, and this hair grows so quick that, seeing me in undress uniform and with that disagreeable ornament on my upper lip, any one would take me for a private."

"Privates, whether of horse or foot, or officers of fortune either, have not your manners nor your figure," said Bernard, with an air of conviction.

"You see I am a man now, a grown man," replied Frederic, smiling. "I shall soon be twenty-one; have had three years' service—in the town, the rank of field-marshal—in imagination; and this uniform, green with red facings, what do you think of it? Is it smart enough?"

"It fits you like a glove; the cut of it suits your figure exactly. What do you say, Marius?"

" I prefer that of the Commander in the portrait, with a red coat and powdered wig."

The old man shrugged his shoulders.

" This is fifty times as handsome," cried he. " Marius, you only like red, which is good for nothing but to enrage bulls. Now this color takes me. I look at it with pleasure. See how that coat opens below to show the vest; see those facings; that breastplate has a manly look, while the King's Guards in their red frocks seem as if they were dancing in a sack. I bet you a crown that Thérésine will be of my opinion."

" The other uniform is richer," said Marius, coldly.

" This is only my undress," said Frederic, much amused by this discussion; " beside my full-dress uniform, this is like the moon to the sun. Now, of course, the Royal Guards no longer wear plumed hats, breeches adorned with ribbons, funnel-shaped shoes, lace cravats, and silken scarfs across the shoulder of an embroidered velvet coat. All that belonged to the time of Louis XIV. and the beginning of the reign of Louis XV. But, nevertheless, when the trumpets sound and our white standard is flung to the breeze, as we pass out of the principal court of the palace of Versailles, squadron by squadron, in full uniform and splendidly mounted, our helmets and swords shining like the sun, our snow-white breeches, our silver spurs glittering at the heels of our long shining boots, the crowd press

round to see us, and often salute us with cries of
' Long live the Queen's Dragoons ! ' "

" I thought all the guards wore the same uniform,"
said Marius.

" Not at all. There are the red gendarmerie, as
you see from my uncle's portrait; the hussars, each
regiment of which wears a different uniform; the
Swiss Guards, with powdered wigs, plumed hats, immense ruffles, parti-colored doublets, and puffed
breeches; the foot-chasseurs, with their helmets of
waxed leather surmounted by a black tassel, their
green dress-coat, and waistcoat of chamois leather:
the Grenadier Guards, who still wear the high bear-
skin caps, a coat of French blue embroidered with
gold, a belt, and long gaiters; the fusiliers, with
cocked hats, blue coats with red facings, and white
brandenburgs clasped a third of the way down; the
blue artillerymen, and all the rest of the army, who
still sport the breeches, white waistcoat, gaiters, and
double shoulder-belts crossed upon the chest. What
are you laughing at, Marius ? "

" Oh, at nothing, Monsieur le Chevalier ; only,
hearing you tell about the Swiss Guards, I could not
help thinking of the masquers who dance round the
Prince of Love in the masquerades at Arles."

" You had better listen and learn," growled Bernard.

" Come, come," cried Frederic, "do not be vexed;
we must always laugh when we can. If the subject

interests you, I will give you many other details
when we are alone; but now, with your permission,
I will proceed with my toilet."

"And I will unsaddle your mare and put her in
the stable, since I can be of no use here," said
Marius, departing at once.

"Must I go too?" asked the old huntsman,
watching his dear Frederic, as he took out a change
of linen and some clothes from his trunk.

"Not at all, my good Bernard; stay and help me
with your advice; at need you can act as valet."

"Since I have the rheumatism, I am not good for
anything but growling and complaining."

"I see, for instance, that you do not spare your
son-in-law."

"The fact is, we do not always agree."

"Yet he seems a good fellow."

"Well, that is true enough; he is a good lad,
and I am not bad; but our dogs do not hunt together."

"Has Thérésine any cause to complain of him?"

"No, thank God! On the contrary, they get on
very well, so far, and seem to understand each other
perfectly."

"Does he drink?"

"Only water."

"Is he idle?"

"No, very industrious."

"Jealous?"

"I would not advise him to try."

"A gambler?"

"He has never touched either cards or dice in his life."

"What fault can you find with him, then?"

"Absolutely none; and yet there is something."

"What can it be?"

"I fear he is too fond of money and not fond enough of you."

"Why do you think so?"

"I do not know."

The young officer burst out laughing in spite of himself. Still seated in the arm-chair, Bernard passed his hand through his gray hair with an anxious look upon his weather-beaten face. Frederic was afraid that he had involuntarily wounded him, and turned the conversation upon hunting. To his great surprise, the old huntsman, whom it was usually so easy to interest in this subject, answered almost in monosyllables. After fruitless endeavors to get him into the vein, the young officer went over and, standing directly in front of him, laid his hand upon his shoulder, saying:

"You have something on your mind, Father Bernard."

"Well, yes, I have a suspicion here," said he, regarding his young master fixedly and striking his own breast; "for some weeks past I am afraid that Marius is a hypocrite."

" That is a bad thought, which it is better to shake off."

" I cannot."

"But what reason have you to suspect him ?"

" Merely a stupid joke, a thoughtless word, that Josiau the bone-setter, who came to set Bernadette the salt-maker's arm, let fall before me."

" What was it ?"

" They were speaking of a lad that came some years ago to gather salt from the marshes on the islands, and who, on his return to Nismes, was arrested for a theft committed at the fair of the Madeleine at Beaucaire, and hanged by order of the présidial." *

" There are thieves everywhere."

" Of course; but this one came to that from being a good workman and an honest lad. So Bernadette said: ' The judges must have been mistaken ; it is impossible that he could have committed such a wicked action.' Nearly all those present, and myself among the number, were of the same opinion; but Josiau said: ' I would put my hand in the fire that the judges were right.' Then Bernadette asked him why, and he replied: ' Sooner or later, believe me, all children whose parentage is unknown go bad, for the devil is with them from the moment of their birth.' "

---

* A magistrate.

" What nonsense! " said Frederic; " and besides, how does that concern Marius ? "

" Then you do not know his history ? "

" What is it ? "

" The story of his birth ? "

" *Ma foi!* no."

" Well, listen.   It is twenty-seven years and a few days since your uncle the Commander was returning one evening on horseback from the Saintes-Maries.   He was alone, but his loaded pistols were in the holster, to be used in case of need.   It was in harvest-time and very warm, so that was why he had made up his mind to travel by night and avoid the flies.   It was after sunset when he reached the marsh of la Sigoulette; the place was quite deserted, and the plain as bare as usual.   The Commander rode along, reading, as is his wont, a book, which he always carries in his pocket, to pass the time. All at once his horse started and shied.   Your uncle passed his book from his right hand to his left, took a pistol, and looked about him, supposing that one of the bulls had escaped from its keeper.   He looked and looked, but saw nothing suspicious; then, returning the pistol to the holster, he put spurs to his horse.   But the horse, instead of advancing, reared and snorted.   There was certainly something.   Any one else would have thought of magic or the presence of some invisible being, but the Commander was not easily frightened.   Seeing nothing before or around him, he looked down on the ground. Almost between the feet of his horse, lying in the dust, was a black bulk, surrounded by a pool of blood. He dismounted, threw the bridle over his arm, and, raising a wretched drugget cloak, discovered the body of a woman, still alive and holding in her arms a poor little child of three or four months old, motionless and covered with blood. What was he to do, alone in the desert ? The charitable gentleman did not hesitate a moment. The Valcarès was close by; he ran thither, filled his hat with the brackish water, bathed the dying woman's face with it, and tried every means of bringing her to consciousness. He strove to raise her, but she, summoning all her strength to keep her hold upon the child, fell back into his arms, murmuring: ' I am dying. Save him ! I give him to you.' She was indeed dying. A blow from a club or some other instrument had fractured her skull, and her body was one mass of bruises.

" Your uncle tried to question her, asking who she was and by whom she had been reduced to such a condition; but she only repeated, her voice growing feebler and more feeble, ' Save my child ! I give him to you.' With these words she expired."

" So that my uncle could find out nothing more ? " asked Frederic.

" Absolutely nothing more," replied Bernard.

" He should have brought the matter before a

magistrate, and caused an inquest to be held, for the woman must have been known in the country."

"No, she was a stranger who had come on foot a few days before to pray at the tomb of the Marys. They could only conjecture that she was accomplishing a vow, because, though on foot, as I said before, she had given abundant alms. Besides, her hands were white and slender and her feet small, and this, together with her dress, showed her to be above the peasant class."

"But why was she murdered, and who could have dealt her such a blow?"

"Some vagrant, no doubt, for the sake of her money, as not a farthing was found upon her. The mounted police, in scouring the country, arrested five or six vagabonds, one of whom had some pieces of gold upon him; he could not explain satisfactorily how they had come into his possession, so he was subjected to the torture. He did not confess, and at last was able to prove that he had been seen at Trinquetaille that very same day. He had probably gone thither to pick pockets during the fair just then going on; so the judges marked him with a fleur-de-lis and sent him to row the king's galleys."

"It is a strange story," said Frederic. "I heard it in a vague way, but thought it was one of those fireside tales which are told in the winter evenings; the more so that neither my mother nor my uncle would reply to any questions concerning it."

"In truth," said Bernard, "the Commander would never speak of it, lest it might injure Marius."

"Yet it was never known to be his story," said Frederic, "for I always heard that he was a native of Avignon."

The old huntsman shook his head.

"Six years after the events I have related," said he, "your uncle brought him from that place, under pretence of training him to be a shepherd at the Commandery. There was a good deal of talk at first, for people do not often take six-year-old shepherds, and show so much interest in them, and care for them as if they were their own children. Before being put to tend sheep, the child was taught to read and write; when he was asked about his parents, he always replied that he only knew an aunt, who had brought him up. This aunt was really his nurse. People had to content themselves with this reply, for, as the Commander had turned away a workman who ventured to call Marius a foundling, they knew that they must hold their tongues."

"At fifteen Marius was made assistant herdsman, and three years after chief; but by that time none would have ventured to question him, for, besides being the master's favorite, he was a robust lad with whom few would care to quarrel; he was a fearless rider, hardy in bearing fatigue, a first-class wrestler, and a splendid bull-tamer, with a pair of fists that made the most audacious respect him."

"I think you are right and that he would not be a very safe person with whom to quarrel," remarked Frederic, all the while continuing his toilet.

"Seeing that, they let him alone," resumed Bernard; "they got accustomed to him. He had a pleasant word for every one, and was hail-fellow-well-met with them all; so they ceased to care who his parents were or whence he came. On his part, he never meddled with the affairs of others, but took care of his own, and, it must be admitted, to some purpose; from chief guardian he became overseer, and in that position was able to indulge his passion for hunting. Skilful in all out-door exercises, he soon became an excellent shot. I had seen little of him before that, but, as we were both overseers and both huntsmen, we were naturally thrown a good deal together, and, though I think he is not straightforward in his disposition, we soon became intimate."

"I remember well," said Frederic, "I made my first shots between you two in a duck-cover on the Valcarès. That is a good while ago, and he was even then a famous huntsman."

"Better for feathers than skins," growled Bernard.

"Yet I have seen him make some havoc among rabbits," said Frederic. "Come, my old comrade, I fear that just now professional jealousy prevents you doing him justice."

"No, Monsieur Frederic, I am telling you the real

truth; a duck on the wing he is sure to take, but he often misses hares or rabbits."

" I do not say that he is as good a shot as you," said Frederic, " but that I would be very glad to be as good a shot as he."

" You are not a bad shot at all," said the old huntsman, with a smile of gratified pride at his pupil's adroit flattery; " and when you come upon a brace of woodcock in the marsh of la Sigoulette, I would rather be in my clothes than in their feathers."

" You are a vile flatterer, Bernard," said Frederic; " but go on with your story."

" Henceforth, then, we often hunted together, but he rarely came into the house; he had his business to attend to, I had mine; and when he sometimes called for me, it was always very early in the morning, so that he merely whistled or knocked at the door of the *Mas*, and waited outside. I came down and we set off. About that time, or a little later, Ma'amselle Germaine returned from school, to spend two months of vacation at the *Mas Rouge*. You may suppose my girl was delighted to see her. They were never apart; every day there was some new pleasure-party, a sail on the river, or a ride to les Saintes or to Arles. When they went to town, it was always with your mother; in the boat I rowed them; but on horseback they were under the special care of the Commander, because Madame was afraid they might meet one of the wild bulls, that often escape when the guardians take them to pasture in the marshes.   All went well till one day a messenger arrived from the Commander, bringing a note for Madame, who sent for me and said:

"'My brother is ill; there is danger of inflammation of the lungs.   Get the carriage ready for me, and have the two ponies saddled besides.   You will accompany us and bring back the horses.'

"'Will Madame be coming back to-morrow?' I asked, 'for, in that case, it would be scarcely worth while to bring the horses back to-night.'

"'God knows when we will come back,' said Madame; 'not for a week at least.   In any case I will let you know.   I shall take Thérésine with me to keep my daughter company and wait upon her. Tell her to come up now and help us to pack.'

"This was the first time that I was separated from Thérésine; it cost me something to let her go, but of course, as long as I knew she could be useful, I took good care not to show any unwillingness.

"The trunks packed, we set out at the appointed time, and reached the Commandery in two hours. Your uncle was in bed with fever, and Marius at Arles, where he had gone for M. Rigal, the doctor. I bade Thérésine, then a well-grown girl, to be very attentive to the ladies, promised to come and see her in two or three days, and, as I knew she was always good and sensible, went home without any

uneasiness. I went back in three days. Libourel
the barber had been brought to bleed the Commander, and the doctor could not pronounce him
out of danger till the ninth day. Thanks be to God,
much more than to the doctor, your uncle was out
of danger before then, but he was a long time coming round, and the ladies were a long time away. I
had a great deal of work in the daytime at the *Mas
Rouge*, and was so busy that I had little time to
think; but at night I was very lonely. Whenever I
could take half a day to myself, I mounted a mare,
and I assure you I did not give the flies much time
to torment her. In an hour and a half or an hour
and three quarters I was at the *Mas Vieux*. Sometimes, when I arrived, hoping to find Thérésine, I
was told:

" ' She is gone out with Mlle. Germaine.'

" ' Where to ?'

" ' To the Rhone.'

" ' *Peste !* it is not easy to guide a boat on that
rapid river. Who handles the oars ?'

" ' Marius. You need not fear; there is no boat-
man like him.'

" ' Very well,' I would say.

" Or it would be:

" ' Thérésine is gone with Mlle. Germaine to visit
the ruins of the monastery of Ulmet.'

" ' That is very far, and the bulls go to pasture
there. Who is with them ?'

" ' Marius.   Do not be afraid; he is the best guardian in Camargue.'

" Or else:

" ' They are gone to the salt-works of Galépion, to see the salt taken up.'

" ' The marsh is not very safe on that side, and they might easily go astray.   Who is their guide ? '

" ' Marius, and he knows the marshes.   There is not a salt-worker who could teach him anything about them.'

" I began to get tired of hearing the perfections of Marius.   It seemed to me an age till the Commander got well.   The doctor was not of my opinion; but your uncle's constitution was victorious over the doctor's medicines and the barber's bleeding.   So, at last, he came back to health, and my daughter to the *Mas Rouge*.   Some months passed. Mlle. Germaine had returned to the convent, Thérésine was busy with her work, and our life had fallen into the old way.   Marius came more seldom even than before.   One day, however, the Commander passed through the garden with his sister.   I was pruning a nettle-tree, and the Commander stopped, and said to me, all of a sudden:

" ' Bernard, how old is your daughter ? '

" I laughed, because I knew very well she was your foster-sister, and I said:

" ' Three months older than M. Frederic.'

"'It is a good age for her to marry,' said he; 'have you thought of it?'

"All the while he was looking at me with a droll expression and Madame was plucking the petals out of a daisy.

"'Not yet, sir,' I answered, 'and I don't think that Thérésine herself has thought of it either.'

"'Well, I have thought of it for both of you,' he said, 'and I have found her a jewel of a husband, who will make her very happy.'

"I could easily guess; I expected every moment to hear:

"'It is Marius; and in all the world she could not find a better.'"

Spite of the emotion with which the old huntsman spoke, Frederic could not help laughing.

"It is easy to see you are not a father," said Bernard, simply.

"I beg your pardon, old comrade. I did not mean to offend you," said Frederic.

Bernard resumed:

"I looked at the Commander frightened-like, and he must have seen it in my eyes, for he said:

"'Come, answer me. I am not going to take your daughter from you. I only want to know if you will consent to give her to a worthy fellow for whom I can answer, and who will, I guarantee, make her happy.'

"'I am ready to do anything that will make her

happy, sir,' I said; 'but I am not the one who is asked in marriage, so I cannot decide.'

" He seemed surprised, and said:

" ' What, it is not the father who decides ? '

" ' I think,' said I, ' with your permission, it is rather she whom it most concerns.'

" He burst out laughing, and, turning to Madame, said:

" ' Sister, did you choose your own husband ? '

" ' I was married at thirteen,' she answered, ' to M. de Marcoiran, who was then fifteen, and whom I had never seen. My father and mother sent word a week before to the convent that I was to come home for the ceremony. On that occasion we were allowed to dine at the table with our parents; after it was over, a maid brought me back to the Visitation nuns, and a lackey escorted my husband to college. We did not see each other again for five years.' "

" That is the way marriages are usually arranged," said Frederic, not at all surprised, " the same with other things. When my mother and uncle decided I was to go into the army, they sent me off to my regiment, instead of to college."

" In your rank of society such things are done, but in ours, Monsieur Frederic, we let the children choose."

" *Ma foi!* I confess that I never thought of such a thing," said Frederic. " If my people want me to

marry, let them find me a wife. They will save me
the trouble of looking for one, and I would just as
soon they chose for me."

"It was a great sacrifice for me to let Thérésine
marry at all, and I wanted her at least to choose a
husband that would suit her. When he saw that
my mind was made up, the Commander said:

"'Since you have that idea, consult her.'

"'I must know his name.'

"'Of course you must. Well, it is Marius, my
huntsman, the overseer of the estate of the *Mas Vieux*.
You know him; he is a good, industrious fellow, and
of irreproachable character. I brought him up myself; and as he has no relations, he will attach himself
much more easily to you than any other you could
find.'

"I thanked the Commander, and promised to
speak to Thérésine.

"I hesitated for three whole days; whenever I
opened my mouth to speak, something seemed to
keep me back. I said to myself, 'It is because his
parentage is unknown;' but I knew very well that I
was jealous of my child's affection. However, I had
to give an answer. So one evening at dinner my
girl noticed that I ate less and drank more than
usual. She remarked it to me in her own sweet
way.

"'I need something to give me courage,' said I.

"Thérésine looked at me with her eyes wide open,

and asked why. I took another glass of wine, and said to her:

" ' You are nearly twenty.'

" ' I am three days past twenty,' she said, smiling.

" I continued:

" ' It is time to think of marrying.'

" She still looked at me, and I did not know what to say next.

" ' Yes, it is time to marry. What have you to say ? '

" ' Nothing at all, father. I am listening to you.'

" ' Answer me, then.'

" ' What do you want me to answer ? You did not ask me anything.'

" ' I said it was time to marry.'

" ' Yes, it is time to marry,' she repeated like an echo.

" ' Is there any one you would like to marry ? ' I said, furious at my own stupidity.

" ' No one,' she said. ' What made you think of it ? '

" ' What ? What ? ' I repeated, ' because it is time.'

" ' Some one has asked me in marriage,' she said, after a pause.

" ' Yes: Marius, of the *Mas Vieux*. Do you want to marry him ? '

" ' I have no wish of my own, father. I will do as you like, for it is my duty to obey you.

" ' Obey me ! But I have not commanded you to do anything. Do as you think best. Reflect on it. I give you an hour.'

" ' An hour is very little,' she said. ' Yet, if you leave me entirely free, I will not need even so much.'

" ' I leave you free.'

" ' Then I will not marry Marius.'

" ' And why ? '

" ' Because I do not want to leave you and my good masters, and because I want to stay at the *Mas Rouge.*' "

" You must have been pleased with this answer," said Frederic.

" You think so, yet it was just the contrary," said Bernard. " Having said that it was time for her to marry, and that if she did not take Marius she would never find as good a husband, I persuaded myself that she ought to accept him. Her answer vexed me.

" ' Have you anything against him ? ' I asked.

" ' Nothing at all,' she said.

" ' Then there is some one you like better ? '

" ' No; if I were to choose, I should prefer him.'

" ' Perhaps you would rather live in Arles, or even Marseilles ? '

" ' I hate the town and love the country.'

" ' You do not think him rich enough ? '

" ' On the contrary, I am not in a position to expect as much.'

" ' *Péchère!* ' I cried. ' Then you have made up your mind never to marry ? '

" ' I do not say that.'

" I could have beaten her, I was so angry.

" ' Well, what *do* you say, then, daughter of the good God ? '

" ' That I would like best of all to stay in the house with you and Mlle. Germaine.'

" ' You have decided, then ? '

" ' I have decided.'

" ' You positively refuse him ? '

" ' Unless you command me to do otherwise, I positively refuse him.'

" ' Then good-night.   I am off shooting.'

" I took my gun, whistled for my dog, and went off. I came in about one o'clock in the morning. I had missed three rabbits, but did not much care. I threw myself on my bed, but never closed an eye. Next day the Commander sent for me into the *salon,* where he was alone with your mother. I could not have been more upset if I had been brought into court. Your uncle questioned me. I told him all that had passed. When I had finished, he shrugged his shoulders and said:

" ' I knew you were stupid, but not quite as stupid as that.'

" I recovered a little then, for I had expected much worse. Your mother laughed, and stole a

glance at me now and again over her work.   The
Commander turned to her and said:

"'What do you think, sister? I suppose with
this fool it is better to leave matters as they are.'

"Madame stopped, rubbed her forehead with her
knitting-needle, and said:

"'I think we may find a way of arranging matters.'

"'How do you mean?'

"'Thérésine refused to leave the *Mas Rouge*, but
she did not refuse to marry Marius.   Let him come
here, and the objection is removed.'

"The Commander made a wry face.   He did not
like to part with his overseer.

"He rose, and walked about, gnawing the end of
his cane.

"I stood there twirling my hat between my hands.

"'Nothing can succeed with such a fool as this,'
said the Commander, crossing his arms and looking
at me.   'It is useless to try.'

"'Will you let me negotiate the affair?' said Madame, in her soft voice.

"'I suppose it would be better,' said he, resuming his walk, and, as he passed me, saying: 'I have
no further need of you.'

"As I went out I met Thérésine, counting the
house-linen, which she always sent to the laundry.

"'Good-day, father,' said she, going on with her
counting.

"At breakfast she spoke of indifferent things.   I
felt like crying out: 'It is time for you to marry.'
Her calmness angered me.

"Two days went by.   One morning I was just
lacing my gaiters to go to the rush-beds of Agon,
for a landowner from la Crau wanted to buy some
slips, when in came Thérésine, as fresh and smiling
as ever.

"'Father,' said she, 'Madame wants you; come
at once.'

"I followed her, one gaiter on my leg, the other
in my hand, for I suspected something, and was not
as tranquil over it as your foster-sister.

"'My brother,' said Madame, 'has consented to
let Marius come here to live with us; your rheumatism prevents you from working as you used; Marius
can help you, and as he has a good disposition you
will get on well together.   I have spoken to the
little one.   It is a good match for her; you would
be wrong to let it escape.   Thérésine understands
all this, since I explained it all to her.   She likes
Marius as well as, or better than, any one else, and
only waits for your consent to pledge herself to
him.'

"Something like a cold hand clutched my heart.
I felt that I turned pale.   But my daughter seemed
pleased, and I knew what a wise and prudent woman
your mother is, so I said:

"'I consent.'

" I never knew before how hard it could be to bring two words out of my throat.

" So that is the story of Marius, and of his marriage with my daughter. The marriage was, however, delayed eight months, because your uncle wanted to keep his overseer for the fall work. Besides, I was in no hurry ; though whenever my daughter saw me looking down a bit, she always said : ' There will be two of us to love and care for you.' It was often on the tip of my tongue to answer : ' You alone were all I wanted.' At last the time came, and we have been together ever since ; but I must admit that they are both so kind to their old father that I have nothing but praise for them. I was even growing to be really fond of Marius, and to feel towards him as if he were my own son, when Josiau let drop those unfortunate words, and they have been ringing in my ears ever since. Tell me, Monsieur Frederic, you who have been in Paris, where there are so many wise people, did you ever hear it said that, sooner or later, foundlings go to the bad ? "

" No, my dear Bernard, it is a stupid lie, in which there is not a word of truth, and you can tell this babbling bone-setter so from me," said Frederic, who was now nearly dressed. " Your son-in-law is a good, honest fellow, and you are very wrong to suspect him. But hush, there is some one coming."

It was Thérésine, who in her clear fresh voice,

as joyous as the song of the lark, called through the
door:

"Come down, Monsieur Frederic, your breakfast
will be cold."

"I am just coming," he answered.

CHAPTER III.

THE RETURN FROM ARLES.

WHILST the whole household at the *Château Rouge*, from Bernard and Marius, Thérésine, the housekeeper, and the old cook, Zounet, down to the shepherds and herdsmen, whose occupations kept them at the farm, were crowding round to greet their young master on his return, a heavy travelling-carriage, which had set out from Arles about the same time that he had, was driving along the road beside the Rhone, and raising on its passage a thick cloud of dust, which could be seen from afar, whitening the trees.

Although certain of having their dresses powdered gray with dust, the three ladies who occupied the vehicle had, on account of the heat, let down the window on the river side. They kept up a lively conversation, from time to time addressing an elde y gentleman who rode beside the carriage. He seemed specially interested in pointing out each village, or rather each habitation, to a fair young girl, whose large blue eyes looked with the greatest curiosity at the strange country, which she was evidently

visiting for the first time.   Just opposite her, for she
had the place of honor beside Madame de Marcoiran,
who had never left off her mourning since her husband's death, sat Germaine in a simple white dress,
confined at the waist by a flame-colored ribbon, similar to that which tied back the thick braids of her
blue-black hair.   Beside her, facing Madame, was a
country gentleman of distinguished appearance, despite the simplicity of his attire, whose face denoted
great energy of character.

If Camargue in the interior presented the appearance of a bare and desolate desert, half sandy, half
marshy, it must be admitted that following the windings of the river there was no trace of this sterility.

The banks were, indeed, fertilized by the stream
and the alluvial nature of the soil.   Oaks, elms,
plantains, and sycamores, amongst which wild vines
hung their verdant garlands, swaying in the breeze,
resembled, with their intertwining branches, the
thickness of their foliage, the majestic height of their
enormous trunks, a virgin forest, giving glimpses in
rare openings of the blue waters wherein their roots
grew, and which had a thick border of stiff, shining
reeds.   From amongst these reeds rose, with great
flapping of wings and harsh, metallic cries, flocks
of wild ducks, blue-headed teal, red flamingoes with
their enormous wings, water-fowl with red beaks,
gray crake folding their long yellow claws under their
wings, or the beautiful kingfisher, who goes as quick as

thought, so that scarcely a glimpse can be caught of his dazzling plumage, sparkling with emeralds and rubies.

Through this ocean of verdure, the thickness of which is almost impervious to the sun's rays, the horses went on noiselessly as in the alleys of a park, and, were it not for the double inconvenience of the mosquitoes, that dart out upon travellers as upon their proper prey, and the almost imperceptible but all-penetrating dust, nothing could be pleasanter than a drive through these charming regions. When, betimes, the forest road, where it grew narrower, left an opening, the eye could perceive, through the high colonnade of trees upon which rests the emerald dome, afar off, on the meadow side, immense fields of grain, green in the spring, but yellow ·ᴧ the summer, when the sun ripens them and the ᴜouth wind stirs their promise-laden wares of gold.

" Do you know, it was a terrible thing to deceive me as you did," said the blond young girl, who was no other than Mlle. de Blésignan, addressing Germaine. " If the Commander had not, so to say, forced my father into bringing me here, I should have gone on thinking Camargue a land of desolation, instead of being, as it is, a real Eden."

" You are making its acquaintance at the most favorable time, my dear Renée," said Germaine, " and I advise you not to judge the cloak by its rich border until you have had time to examine its texture more closely."

"It is impossible that Providence should have given so rich a golden fringe to an inferior stuff."

"Yet such is the case, fair lady," said the Commander, gallantly, "and the border of Camargue reminds me of the ingenious allegory of one of our poets, who represents the lame Vulcan trying on, on his own black person, the girdle of his wife, the goddess of beauty, which was so dazzlingly white that it was said to be of sea-foam."

As may be seen, the Commander prided himself on his choice language and knowledge of literature. Well pleased with his allusion, he drew himself up in his saddle, reined in his horse, and, resuming the third position, according to the manner of the *parfait cavalier français*,* took a large pinch of Spanish snuff from his box, lightly shaking off with his little finger a few grains that fell upon his spotless linen neckerchief.

Madame de Marcoiran conversed the while with the Marquis de Blésignan, fanning herself gently all the time. The noble seigneur of Nyons, though an intimate friend of the Commander, did not, like him, plume himself upon his gallantry, so that their conversation, though more simple in form, was much more interesting, for it turned upon the politics of the day. It was naturally of a serious and even despondent tone. Certainly, so far there was

---

* Perfect French rider.

nothing to foreshadow the fearful excesses of '93, but the political horizon was singularly overcast, and gave little hope for the future. An ardent royalist, the Marquis was in favor of extreme measures.

"The King is too good," he repeated, emphasizing his words by tapping on the ivory knob of his stick; "yes, far too good. With all these agents of reform there is but one means to take."

"What is that?" inquired Madame.

"The whip of Louis XIV., Madame. I repeat, the whip."

"That might have succeeded in his time," said Madame, "but we have made so much progress since then."

"Progress in insolence, insubordination, revolt, corruption," said M. de Blésignan. "That's what it is to give free rein to these so-called philosophers, these shameless pamphleteers, who mock at every sentiment of honor, patriotism, religion, decency, and who, with their licentious writings, have brought the country to the verge of infamy. Of course these encyclopædists are masters of the French language and may have a great deal of learning, but they have done incalculable harm with their absurd and irreligious philosophy."

"Their novels have done even more harm," sighed Madame de Marcoiran; adding immediately, "When I say novels, I mean such as l'Émile or the

Nouvelle Héloïse, the only two, indeed, which I was ever tempted to read. As for those of Crébillon and the rest, you must understand that I scarcely know them by name."

" A noble and virtuous lady like Madame de Marcoiran," said the Marquis, " cannot be open to such a suspicion. So white a hand never grovelled in the mire."

" The worst of it is," said the lady, " that the books of which I speak are so well written that. though an upright mind must condemn the opinions of the author, it is nevertheless carried away by the charm of his style, and by that warmth which unconsciously influences—for instance, in reading Rousseau's confession of the *Vicaire Savoyard*. Do you not agree with me ?"

" Most certainly, Madame," replied M. de Blésignan, somewhat hastily, for he was anxious to escape further questioning on a subject on which he was none too well posted, considering that the only writer he knew was the author of the *Maison Rustique*. " This Rousseau," he continued, " corrupt and vicious as we know him to have been, had at least the excuse of being mad, as mad as many who are in the lunatic asylums."

" He has not the wit of Voltaire," said Madame, " but far more generosity of feeling."

" He might easily have that," cried the fiery Marquis, upon whom the name of Voltaire produced

much the same effect that a red rag does upon a
bull. "This M. de Voltaire, though a scion of nobility, a gentleman of His Majesty the King of
France, has a soul of mud. Base wretch that he is,
he, a man of rank, allowed himself to be beaten by
the lackeys of the King of Prussia; he, a Frenchman,
professed himself an admirer of his ' great Frederick,'
the mortal enemy of France, and applauded his fatal
victory at Rosbach; he, a Christian, played the de-
votee at Fernay, and appeared in Paris as the insulter
of God; he, a gentleman, dragged through the mire
the name of a woman specially raised up by Providence to save our country, and who died a martyr
to her heroism. He is the most abominable rascal
that ever lived, and I blush to think that the Pari-
sians should have placed a crown of gold upon the
venomous and contemptible creature's head, when
they should have put a rope around his neck and
dragged him to the pillory for high treason against
honor, against the nation, and against all majesty,
both human and divine."

"Father, father, do not get excited," said Renée
in a low voice, at the same time turning supplicating
eyes upon the Marquis.

"Do not get excited!" said he, rapping so violently with his cane upon the floor of the carriage
that Madame hastily withdrew her feet from their
perilous position. "Then let me hear no more of
this manikin, this scoundrel, this rascal, who, by his

life and writings, is a disgrace to the nobility and a
corrupter of the people.''

Seeing that by her interference she had only
thrown oil on the fire, Renée looked at Germaine,
as if asking her help.

It was, however, the Commander who came to her
rescue. He bent down to the open window, and
cried out in a half-joking, half-ceremonious tone:

'' By Heaven ! I never thought that my old carriage would be transformed into Olympus.''

No one understanding the allusion, every one was
silent and looked at him in surprise.

'' I was perfectly aware,'' he said, addressing
Renée, '' that I was escorting the golden-haired
Venus, but I did not know that I was also to assist,
like the gods of Homer, at a conversation between
the irascible Mars and the wise Minerva.''

'' So that I am the only mortal in the company,''
said Germaine, gayly.

'' You are too modest, fair niece, for I am of opinion that you worthily represent, on this occasion,
the nymph Egeria.''

This said, the gallant horseman again drew himself
up, and again rewarded his own amiability by per-
mitting himself a pinch of that refreshing substance,
the color of which he had adopted in his garments,
namely, snuff. This species of wit, which now
seems to us at once pedantic and antiquated, was
at that time much in vogue; and the ex-officer of

the king's household had won thereby the reputation of being among the most agreeable men who frequented the then very aristocratic *salons* of the town of Arles.

Renée rewarded him with a gracious smile, less perhaps of admiration than of gratitude; but whatever were the young lady's feelings, she had attained the desired result, and her father, ashamed of his late impetuosity, profited by the opportunity to escape from the political and literary arena into which he had so imprudently allowed himself to be drawn. The conversation, interrupted by the Commander's last sally, now remained in a state of apparent indecision as to what subject should be mooted next, when Germaine, putting her head out of the window, cried:

" Montlong ! I did not think we were there yet."

" What is Montlong ? " asked Renée.

" The last *mas*, or, to express myself more correctly, the last farm, from which we can see the Rhone," answered the Commander, pointing with his whip to a small isolated house, the red roof of which was alone perceptible through the foliage.

" Yes," added Germaine, leaning back in the carriage, " you see that deep ditch which, on separating from the river, becomes a round pool: that is what we call the little *roubine* of Montlong, which will lead us by the marsh of Grand-Mar to the Valcarès,

and to the *Mas Rouge*. Open your eyes wide, for
in a few minutes we will be in Camargue proper."

" The river road or trimmings were so beautiful,"
said Renée, " that I am eager to see the texture of
the uniform."

" The texture of the uniform is coarse," said Germaine, " and the color light gray; but it has at least
the merit of not being like what we see everywhere
else."

The carriage made a sudden turn; the trees no
longer obscured the view; fields of grain still green,
though now in the ear, and beyond them the plain,
flat, bare, immense, stretched out before the eye.
Germaine looked at Renée.

" One would think it was the sea," replied Renée,
in a low voice.

" How do you like the sea, then ? " said Germaine.

" It is very sad, but very beautiful," said Renée.

" Do you really think it beautiful ? "

" Most beautiful," said Renée.

" Camargue should have put on its festal garb to
receive you, and changed its dust into verdure," said
the Commander, " lest it frighten your beautiful eyes
by the sad spectacle of its nudity."

" Oh, no; I prefer the desert, which is really magnificent," said Renée. " Does it not seem as if a
cloud of gold were floating over its immensity ? "

" Alas ! it is not the golden cloud with which the
divine Homer enshrouded his Olympus," said the

Commander, "and you will presently discover that these atoms floating in the rays of the sun are but fine dust, infested with a legion of mosquitoes. Mosquitoes and dust are, indeed, the two plagues against which it is almost impossible to protect ourselves."

" Against dust there is soap," said Renée.

" And against the mosquitoes vinegar," said Germaine, " which I, however, never use."

" Since you are impervious to their stings," said Renée, laughing, " I may also be preserved if you mention that I am your kinswoman."

" Oh, they will not believe me."

" Really ? "

" You have blue eyes, mine are black; your hair is fair, mine is as dark as dark can be; and in short, my dear, we are not of the same stuff."

" Now I should have said just the contrary," said Renée.

Mlle. de Marcoiran took Renée's white hand and compared it with her own brown one.

" Look," she said, " is the stuff alike ? "

" Mlle. de Blésignan is of satin," remarked the Commander, courteously.

" And I, of taffeta," said the laughing and guileless Germaine, with her usual sprightliness.

" The two stuffs are of equal value," cried M. de Blésignan, in imitation of his friend.

" I thank you for my daughter." said Madame de

Marcoiran, casting a glance at Germaine which
seemed to say, " I am sure of it."

" It may be so," said Germaine, " but nevertheless the mosquitoes are sure to give you the prefer-
ence, my dear Renée."

" They have, then, a predilection for satin ? "

" Not exactly; but they have the same taste as
the ogres of the fairy-tales: they like new flesh.
Having frequently partaken of me, who am their
compatriot, they would like to change the bill of
fare and try you."

The horses were meanwhile going at a good pace,
with grain-fields on either side of them, and raising as
they went myriads of locusts.   One of these creatures,
in his dizzy flight, grazed Renée's face with his scaly
body and dashed himself against the carriage-window.

" Oh, the horrid beast ! " cried Renée, " how he
frightened me ! "

" The third plague of our dear Camargue," said
her cousin, who had caught the insect and given it to
the Commander.

" That plague is a familiar one to me," said Renée.
" We have locusts in the fields at Nyons and in the
thatch of the houses.   But if plague it be, it is at
least a harmless one."

" Certainly," said the Marquis; " if the mosquitoes
are not more to be feared, we are not in great danger,
for I do not believe that a locust ever did harm to
any one.   What do you say, M. de Forton ? "

But the Commander had all at once grown silent
and thoughtful. He was examining with the greatest attention the prisoner which his niece had caught.
Hearing himself thus directly addressed, he roused
himself, and said, with a gravity which the occasion
scarcely seemed to demand:

"I am not of your opinion, my excellent friend.
These little beasts, whom you think so innocent, do
not find equal favor with me; they have too often
made us, and still continue to make us, feel that of
all our enemies they are the most to be feared."

The Marquis burst out laughing. He thought it
was a joke, much enhanced by the jester's solemn
air.

"You must be terrified," he said, addressing Madame.

"When they appear at this season, there is great
reason to fear for the harvests," replied Madame,
gravely.

"It would be hard for an insect of that size to
destroy a single blade of wheat," said the Marquis.

"Yes, at its present size, I grant you," said the
Commander; "but in eight or ten days from now
the young locusts will be treble that size and the
wheat will be still in the ground."

"You really think they can injure the grain?"
said Renée.

"Why, in an hour," said Germaine, "they can
destroy a whole field."

" Too late, Mademoiselle," cried Renée. " When we were at Saint Praxeda, you used to describe Camargue to me in all sorts of colors, and I believed you; but now that I am grown up I am not quite so credulous."

" It is a *gigantea*," said M. de Forton, throwing the insect away; " the most dangerous species. Our harvests will be ruined if God does not help us."

Then he rode on for some minutes in silence, till, approaching the driver, Renée heard him say:

" Jean-de-Dieu, is Marius at the *Château Rouge ?* "

" Yes, sir."

" Good ! On arriving I shall send him at once to Arles, to let the consuls know that we are threatened with a plague of locusts, and that it is necessary to send soldiers here to attack them before they become too numerous."

" It might be well, too," said the coachman, " to send some of the guardians to collect the people of the farms, and to warn the post-stations at Peccaix, Sylvéréal, and les Saintes, that all these vermin must be exterminated; they are already so numerous that several hundred huntsmen will be needed to destroy them."

Renée looked at Germaine in amazement. She could not believe her ears. Besides the improbability that a man like M. de Forton would amuse himself in keeping up a joke of this nature, with no other object than to mystify the daughter of an intimate friend, she could not suppose that there was an understanding between him and his coachman for the same end. Yet the idea of calling out regiments and convoking peasants to give battle to swarms of locusts seemed to her an utter impossibility. She resolved to make a clean breast of her perplexity to Madame de Marcoiran, and asked her, not without hesitation, to explain what she had heard.

"I am sure these precautions must astonish you, my dear," said Madame, "but locusts, especially of that species like the one you have just seen, when they attain their full development, which is in about eight or ten days, become so strong that in one bite they can cut off a blade of wheat, and so voracious, as well as so numerous, that in an hour or two they can strip the trees of their foliage, or devour the harvests of a large field. When I first came to Camargue after my marriage, and saw these insects for the first time, like you I could not believe in their devastating power, and considered all that I heard about them as vulgar fables. Alas! I learned to my cost that I had made a mistake in regarding as false what was only too true."

"Have you, then, suffered from their ravages?" asked Renée.

"Not once, but a dozen times. Every year, in fact, at the time of their appearance I have to spread nets all over my garden to preserve my dear flowers."

" That these locusts can destroy young tender heads of salad I can understand," said the Marquis, " and I have heard that in the more isolated portions of Africa they commit extraordinary depredations. I was told by a Father of Mercy who came to collect for the redemption of captives that they are generated from the sand heated by the rays of the sun in those vast deserts, where shortly after a wind arises and carries them off in the form of clouds. But here—"

" This is Africa on a small scale, Marquis; there is a desert likewise scorched by a fiery sun, and likewise swept by terrible winds, the power of which you may soon have an opportunity of testing."

" So that even here, Madame, those insects can ravage several acres of cultivated land ? "

" They do more than that here, Monsieur."

" How is that ? "

" When an army of locusts goes out from Camargue, it crosses the Rhone, beside which we have been driving, ravages la Crau, proceeds as far as Beaucaire, carries the town by assault, and, continuing its march, which no power can arrest, lays siege to Montfrin."

" I would very much like to know the date and other details of that unparalleled campaign," said M. de Blésignan, repressing a strong inclination to laugh, " and I would be very grateful to my most learned friend the Commander, who has written with such scrupulous fidelity the history of the King's household troops, if he would give us an account of this expedition, which must have been anterior to the dominion of the Greeks and Romans."

"I am at your service, Marquis," said the Commander, "unless the ladies would prefer some other topic."

"Oh, I beg of you, let us hear it, Monsieur," said Renée.

"With the understanding," said her father, "that history has its origin in fable, and that the Church does not oblige us to believe it."

"I can show you in my study," said the Commander, "some copies taken from authentic documents in the archives of the consulate of Beaucaire, and certified as exact copies by the secretary."

"Exact copies of what?"

"Of the original documents, which are not more than a hundred and fifty years in existence."

"And which are in the archives of the consulate?"

"As I have already told you."

"Your word carries so much weight that I bow to it," said the Marquis. "But permit me one objection; if—"

"Oh, father, I beg of you," said Renée, "let Monsieur de Forton begin his story; you can discuss the matter afterwards."

"Obedience to the ladies," said M. de Forton, gravely raising his three-cornered hat. "We shall discuss it, documents in hand, at some future time. I will now begin.   Jean-de-Dieu, walk the horses."

The coachman obeyed the injunction, and the Commander, having taken a gum-drop from his *bon-bonnière* to clear his voice, paused a moment to collect his thoughts.

" You are really anxious to hear this story ? " said Germaine to Renée, whose eyes were fairly sparkling with impatience.   Her only answer was to put her finger to her lips, for the Commander was about to begin.

" The island of Camargue, most honored ladies," he began, " was formed, as you know, like its neighbor, that of la Crau, by earth brought hither through inundations of the Rhone, or by sand which the fury of the wind had torn from the river-banks.   Although neighbors, these two sisters do not resemble each other in the least.   Whilst in la Crau the soil is almost entirely hidden by a bed of pebbles, between which shoots up a fine grass, serving as pasture for innumerable flocks of sheep, which wander over these stony plains, Camargue cannot boast the smallest pebble, and all stones used in the construction of houses are brought here from a distance.

" This light soil, impregnated as it is with salt, and in most parts rebellious to all culture, offers a vast field of operations for the locusts; they lay their eggs there every autumn without fear that they will be destroyed by the plough.

" The inundations are what they have to dread; but when the winters are exceptionally dry, so that the river does not overflow in the spring, the sun heats the sand, and hatches the eggs in such quantities that in a few days the earth is covered with young insects, scarcely larger than ants. They grow quickly, and proceed in countless swarms to wherever they can find the first food, by means of which they develop, and strengthen their wings. It is only then that they show their voracity and enter upon a campaign. Early in the last century, about 1611-12, the winter and spring were particularly dry, and consequently followed by very early heat, under the influence of which, in all the dried-up marshes, there was a formidable hatching of locusts, who, favored by the temperature, rapidly attained development. A few days sufficed in which to eat up all the grass within their reach; then, incited by hunger, they passed along the river-bank, leaving behind them, instead of rich verdure such as you have just seen, a bare and devastated territory, which seemed as if a conflagration had swept over it. You know that Camargue is in the form of a triangle, the head of which—that is to say, the narrowest point—is near Arles. It was in this narrow space that their ever-advancing army finally encamped. The breadth of the river no doubt saved Arles from the terrible visitation, but the smaller branch of the Rhone could not protect Trinquetaille. The locusts, impelled by hunger and favored, probably, by the wind, rose with a loud noise of wings, and flew over to the other side of the river, where they recommenced their ravages, proceeding in the direction of Beaucaire.

" The Fair of St. Madeleine, which is held every year in that town, was just then going on and extended around the walls the whole length of the Rhone. Bales of merchandise from the Levant, from Italy, Spain, and various parts of France were heaped up in the streets, in the squares, and in that temporary town which the farmers had constructed without the walls. There was a profusion of all materials, and likewise of provisions; besides hay for the beasts of burden, grain, which the porters unloaded from the vessels, and flour, freshly sifted, from the mills of Tarascon.

" Amid all this tumult and the unusual bustle produced by a large concourse of strangers, every one busy with his own affairs, mounted messengers rode post-haste from Trinquetaille to warn the municipal authorities that the enemy was marching upon Beaucaire.

" The locusts had never penetrated that far before. Yet the authorities had often heard of their ravages, and now sent out some reliable men to observe the movements of the invading army and see for themselves if the danger were real. Two days were given them in which to make their report to the council.

" They returned in a few hours, pale with horror

and scarcely able to relate what they had seen. It was not, they said, an invasion, but a living inundation, rolling towards the town with a confused, rumbling sound, caused by the thousands and thousands of insects, who pursued their work of destruction as they came. A few minutes sufficed to reduce a tree laden with foliage to a mere skeleton, from the branches of which poured forth swarms of these creatures, eager to continue their ravages. The enemy was scarcely a league from the town; there was not a moment to be lost. The tocsin sounded from every church, the clarion in every street, announcing with flourish of trumpets to all that those who had merchandise which might be damaged must hasten to enter the city limits, as the gates were about to be closed. The garrison was placed under arms; the major in command during the time of the fair doubled the guards, had the guns loaded, and cannon set up in the direction of the attack. Vessels laden with flour or grain pushed off from the shore, and went to anchor in mid-stream, while the population of the town gathered upon the walls to await the approach of the foe. They had not long to wait. Soon a long gray line could be distinctly traced upon the horizon; it was advancing with the regularity of the tide upon a level beach.

" All at once the last tree in the avenue shivered, as if blown by the wind; a few moments elapsed, and it remained bare and black, while the second

and the third, and all the elms, successively underwent the same process of transformation, resembling
somewhat that of tapers which the extinguisher puts
out, one by one, when the service in church is over.
The multitude looked on in terror; but the gray line
was now quite close to them, and behind it, farther
than eye could reach, was a vast cloud obscuring
fields and meadows. One hope remained to the
owners of cabins outside the walls; this was the obstacle presented to the enemy by the navigation canal,
which cut them off from the town, and from which
the drawbridge had been removed.

" When they reached the bank, the first batallions
actually hesitated and seemed disconcerted; but behind them came a famished horde that passed over
their heads and, spreading their scaly wings, crossed
the canal, over which they hovered like a thick, dark,
moving cloud. One portion of them now settled
upon the meadows and the other swarmed about the
high walls of the town, which presently they began to
climb.

" Their imminent peril roused the inhabitants from
their stupor; each seized branches, brooms, sticks, or
poured boiling water upon the assailants. The cannon
roared, the drums beat, the noise was tremendous,
the slaughter terrible; but still the cloud came on,
and the locusts mounted higher and higher, making
their peculiar noise. This went on till the inundation had crept up to the summit of the ramparts and

deluged the town, dividing into streams and rushing through every street.

" Thus was Beaucaire taken by the locusts in the month of July, 1612, under the reign of the Most Christian Prince Louis, thirteenth of the name," con-cluded the narrator, bowing a second time.

" Oh, Monsieur, do me the favor to tell what hap-pened next!" cried Renée, who was much interested in this recital.

" Alas ! fair damsel, what too often happens in towns taken by assault," said the Commander. " The victors gave themselves up to pillage; they invaded the houses and shops, devoured all cloths and wool-len goods, poisoned the wells, spoiled provisions, in-fected the air, caused an epidemic, which happily had no very serious consequences, and after an occupa-tion of three or four days, during which fearful dam-age was done, finally left Beaucaire by the opposite wall, to march upon the town of Montfrin."

" Of which the locusts, no doubt, likewise gained possession."

"" No, Mademoiselle," said the Commander, smil-ing at the young girl's innocent curiosity; " the Mont-frinois were at once braver and more fortunate than their neighbors of Beaucaire. Seeing the approach of the invading army, they marched against them; every one took up arms, old men, women, and chil-dren. The carnage, lasting for three days, was ter-rible; yet so great was the number of assailants that they would finally have won the day, had not a violent storm, accompanied by a terrific wind, precipitated into the Rhone every variety of these ferocious locusts, from the *gigantea*, or giant, to the blue locust, which is the smallest of all." *

" My God, Monsieur, I hope that they will not be so terrible this year," said Renée, deeply moved.

" I hope so too, fair lady; but as it is written, ' Heaven helps those who help themselves,' I have, as you may have heard, taken precautions against their inroads which will be of great utility."

" Instead of other amusements, my dear," said Madame to the young guest, " we will give you a locust-hunt."

" At which I will be present," cried M. de Blésignan, ever ready to excite himself about nothing, " and I will give them no quarter. I, who thought

---

* Though great accuracy of detail is not usually demanded from a novelist, yet, as we pretend to give a true picture of Camargue in this book, we feel bound to remark that all that is here said of the locusts is confirmed by many authentic documents preserved in the archives of the town of Beaucaire, such as consultations among the consuls, the reports of the treasurers, and the like. We may add that in 1513 swarms of these insects in a few hours ravaged eight thousand acres in the Arles territory, and that in the same year the consuls of Arles, Beaucaire, Tarascon, and Marseilles proclaimed a reward of twenty cents for every pound of eggs gathered. Sufficient eggs were brought them to have produced six thousand millions of these insects. Despite the precautions now taken, and the cultivation of portions of the land, which prevents them arising in such numbers, we have ourselves seen, on the 24th of May, 1875, whole companies of soldiers setting out from Arles or Marseilles to combat these insects.—*Author's Note.*

them so harmless and innocent. That is the way many people deceive us in this world."

Madame smiled behind her fan: with a man of this temperament it was impossible to converse calmly or correctly.

"We will go together," said Germaine in a low voice to her friend. "Do you ride?"

"I often ride at Nyons," said Renée.

"Very well; then I can promise you a treat."

"The pleasure of this hunt will have the added charm of novelty."

"If you are brave," said Germaine, "I will also take you to the *ferrades* and *muselades*."

"What are they?"

"You shall see. Contests with bulls, and all that. I will tell you no more."

"Germaine, like the true Camarguaise that she is," said Madame, "enjoys them beyond measure; but I doubt, my dear Renée, whether you will take the same pleasure in these somewhat savage amusements."

"We shall also make an excursion to the seashore, visit the village of Aigues-Mortes, fish, sail upon the Valcarès, and look in upon our friends the salt-workers."

"Who are the salt-workers?"

"People who gather the salt and work in the salt-works."

"So many and such varied pleasures, my dear!" said Renée.

" Ah, activity is a necessity here. We should be very much bored if we were not occupied; in cities amusements seek us; here we must seek them."

" With you I shall not be bored for an instant; besides, this country has a charm which attracts me already. Oh, look there! it seems as if it had rained down sugar."

" Where ? "

" There, on the banks of those streams."

" Ah, yes; that is the summer snow. In a moment or two you will see a vast expanse covered with it."

" Does it snow here in summer ? "

" Certainly; but this snow, instead of falling from heaven, comes up out of the earth: it is simply salt."

" Whence does it come ? "

" These lands are usually covered with salt water in the winter," said Madame; " the water sinks into the earth, and when the summer comes, the sun absorbs the damp, and by certain natural laws which I cannot explain to you the salt is again attracted to the surface, which it powders. Look on this side, and you will see enough of it."

" It certainly has the appearance of great sheets of unmelted snow," said Renée; " and it would even seem frozen hard, for the sun makes it sparkle like diamonds." ·

" Camargue is doing all it can to receive you worthily," said the Commander; " first it offered you flowers and verdure, now it spreads under your feet a white mantle strewn with pearls, rubies, and diamonds."

" I am very grateful to it," said Renée, " but I confess that I would be afraid to venture upon that shining carpet."

" Why, my dear ?" asked Germaine, in surprise.

" For fear I should sink."

" At the most your feet would leave their imprint on that brilliant and brittle surface."

" And never yet would the Sansouire have retained a more charming impression," said M. de Forton, who was at his twentieth pinch of snuff, and consequently at his twentieth compliment. Truth to tell, his compliments had but little effect upon the young girl to whom they were addressed. Leaning out of the carriage, she devoured everything with her eyes, asking explanations of her companions, who enjoyed her astonishment. All at once she gave an exclamation of delight at sight of a superb stream, the blue waters of which, stirred by a gentle breeze, shook its crown of reeds, which shone like sword-blades in the rays of the sun, while it lay like a velvet mantle embroidered with stars of fire.

On the banks of this stream, which flowed on to the sea in a verdant grove of trees gracefully outlined against the sky, was a large white house, at once retiring and coquettish.

" We have arrived," said Germaine. " There is the Valcarès, and there the château."

CHAPTER IV.

LES SAINTES MARIES.

GREAT was the surprise of the Chevalier Frederic when, informed at the last moment of the arrival of the carriage, he had seen his uncle the Commander opening the carriage-door and giving his hand to a tall and beautiful young girl, dressed with elegant simplicity, who was the first to alight from the vehicle.

He did not recognize Mlle. de Blésignan at first, and stood motionless till a mischievous smile from Thérésine, who, a few steps behind him, was enjoying the dramatic effect which her discretion had produced, revealed the secret to him. He promptly recovered himself, with that ease which comes from intercourse with the world, and went forward to meet and offer his compliments to the gracious visitor.

Certainly his compliments, which were quite impromptu, were offered with delightful courtesy. The way in which he kissed Renée's hand was so correct, and his greeting to the old Marquis so perfectly *en règle*, that M. de Forton, who had been somewhat disconcerted by the unexpected appearance of his nephew, whom he had been wont to call "the savage of Camargue," suddenly lost his anxious air, and said in a low voice to Madame:

"See how much the Chevalier is changed for the better!"

Unfortunately, both Madame and Germaine were too much engrossed with the joy of seeing Frederic again to give a thought to etiquette, and, instead of responding to his greeting by a ceremonious reverence, they threw themselves, each in turn, into his arms, embracing him with a tenderness which threatened to spoil this happy beginning.

And the worst was to come; for when the Commander strove to explain this breach of conventionality to his old friend the Marquis, by explaining that if Frederic had behaved thus unceremoniously in presence of Mlle. de Blésignan, it was because he had not seen his people for years, M. de Blésignan cried out:

"*Cornebleu!* my boy, we are not at Trianon or Versailles; and being in the country, the least we can do is to act as if we were in the country. God be praised! I like to see the lad give his mother and sister a hearty kiss. It shows he has some heart in his composition and some blood in his veins."

"You are indulgent, Marquis," said the Commander, "and I thank you for it, but Mlle. de Blésignan may be offended."

"Renée offended! Oh, do not fear, my dear Commander. She has been accustomed in the mountains to plenty of liberty and freedom from restraint, and I can assure you in advance that she will be delighted to find herself in a house where etiquette does not impose its cold and narrow formalities."

M. de Forton made no reply, but he heaved an involuntary sigh of regret that M. de Blésignan should attach so little importance to the laws of good breeding and true politeness.

Meanwhile the Queen's Dragoon, less negligent than his uncle supposed, had already returned to the young lady, and offered his arm to lead her into the *Mas Rouge*.

After a few minutes' conversation in the drawing-room under the eyes of a whole gallery of ancestors hanging upon the walls, above the sofas and armchairs embroidered by a long succession of noble châtelaines, the company dispersed; the Commander to escort the Marquis to his apartment, Germaine to bring Renée to that which Thérésine had prepared for her near her friend's, while Madame de Marcoiran, desiring to have a few moments alone with her son, went out with him to walk in the quiet alleys of the garden.

Naturally they spoke at first of his health, his sojourn at Versailles, his journey home, and in fact all that, most nearly concerning the young man, most interested his mother.

At this moment, however, the Queen's Dragoon

would fain have given another turn to the conversation; he knew all about himself, and though he
certainly loved his regiment, and would not willingly
have exchanged his uniform for a civilian's dress, nor
his brilliant life at Versailles for a very prolonged stay
at Camargue, whose duck-covers were not so near his
heart as he had declared, probably in all sincerity,
to old Bernard, he did not care to talk of these things
just then.

For, having been set at liberty for a few months,
he was eager to enjoy his new life, to spread his
wings, as it were, forget his battalion, his superior
officers, and the court, to be merged once more in
the daring hunter of old. Such were his feelings on
getting home; and now his curiosity had a fresh
stimulus. The appearance of Renée upon a balcony
overlooking the garden gave him an opportunity to
put a few questions in his turn. Leaning upon the
railing, Renée and Germaine chattered together like
two pretty magpies; their animated conversation, interrupted by bursts of fresh, sweet laughter, caused
Madame to look up.

" I did not know that Mlle. de Blésignan was coming here," said Frederic, looking at the two pretty
heads, one dark, one fair, framed by a flowering
vine. " Why did you not tell me ? "

" I myself knew only about a week ago," said Madame. " Your uncle told me of it when he came
back from Avignon, where he had gone on business."

" Does M. de Blésignan live in Avignon now ? "

" No, he has not left Nyons, but he was in Avignon that day, and your uncle met him there. You know they are old friends."

" They were in the Household Troops together," said Frederic.

" Yes, and they had not seen each other for a long time," continued Madame. " So my brother insisted that the Marquis should come to spend some days at the Commandery."

" M. de Blésignan accepted the invitation ? "

" On the contrary, he pleaded that he could not leave his daughter alone."

" ' Bring her with you, then,' said my brother.

" ' She would be very homesick, alone in a strange place,' said the Marquis."

" She knew my sister," interrupted Frederic.

" So your uncle told him, and reminded him of the slight relationship between the families. This rather staggered the Marquis, and he said:

" ' Well, I do not positively refuse your invitation, and I shall certainly pay you a visit as soon as possible.'

" ' But, my dear Blésignan, here is the very opportunity,' said the Commander. ' This is the most favorable season to make a voyage of discovery into the desert. The country will be still green, there will not be too much wind, and the heat will be

moderate. Mlle. de Blésignan has never seen Camargue, which is most original and has a peculiar
charm of its own. My sister and my niece will be
agreeable companions for her. When she is tired of
the desert, we shall make excursions to the many
curious places that serve us as frontier towns. Arles,
celebrated for its Roman monuments, the beauty of
its women and their picturesque costume; Saint-
Gilles, with its mediæval ruins, its crypt, its beautiful front, and the famous spiral of Saint-Gilles, a
staircase so marvellous in execution that no one can
be made a master mason without having studied it;
Aigues-Mortes, slumbering since the time of the Cru-
sades behind its magnificent walls, modelled upon
those of Dalmatia; its celebrated tower of Constance,
built by Saint Louis just before sailing for Palestine;
the famous monastery of Franquevaux and Psalmody,
contemporary with Charlemagne ; Beaucaire, where
its unrivalled fair will open in a few weeks. You will
see the gathering-in of the harvests, cutting of grasses,
ferrades and *muselades*, and a hunt such as you have
never seen.' In a word," concluded Madame, "he
opened our jewel-case and displayed all our treasures
at once."

" Not quite all," said Frederic, " for, in your esti-
mation, he passed over in silence the most precious
of jewels."

" What is that ? "

" Les Saintes."

" No, your uncle held that out as a final induce-
ment, but still his friend hesitated, saying:

" ' Perhaps. I will speak to her about it. In a
few weeks we might—'

" ' In a few weeks will be too late,' cried your
uncle. ' While seeking an opportunity you will miss
the best one of all.'

" ' What is that ? '

" ' The famous pilgrimage of les Saintes, which
takes place on the twenty-fifth of May.'

" ' Ah, it is true. I promised to take her there.'

" ' Well, now is the time to keep your promise.
We will go together from the *Mas Rouge* to the tomb
of the Marys, which is only a pleasant drive. Come,
it is agreed. Be at Arles on Sunday, the twenty-
third, and we will meet you there.'

" ' Urgent business keeps me at Arles over to-
morrow.'

" ' Then Monday at latest; the journey to Arles
will take a few hours at the most; there is nothing
to prevent you, once your business is done, from
sleeping there; next day we can bring you over to
the *Château Rouge*.'

" M. de Blésignan, dislodged from his last intrench-
ment, gave in, and that is how they came here so
unexpectedly."

" Of course you are all going to les Saintes to-
morrow ? "

" All," said Madame, " for I suppose you will be of the party."

" Most certainly; with the greatest pleasure," said Frederic. " Mlle. Renée will probably stay some weeks here ? "

" Some days, at all events. Would you have recognized her ? "

" Yes and no. Her features are the same, and yet she is wonderfully changed."

" How long is it since you saw her ? "

" Nearly six years. It was while she was at the convent; but then she wore a black uniform, and, as well as I can remember, seemed delicate, pale, sickly, and very small."

" That is not surprising when you consider that she was then scarcely twelve years old. At that age it is not very easy to guess what a young girl will be."

" Now she has a splendid figure, a queenly carriage, a look of distinction which many of the court ladies might envy, perfectly regular features, and exquisite golden hair."

" I like her appearance very much," said Madame; " but what pleases me most of all is her perfect simplicity, frankness, and amiability."

" Her blue eyes have not the spirit in them," said Frederic, " that Germaine's dark ones have. When Germaine is animated her eyes shine like stars."

Their conversation was interrupted at that moment

by Thérésine, who came to inform them that the
curate of Notre Dame d'Amour was waiting in the
drawing-room. The good priest, hearing of the return of his former pupil, had come in all haste to see
him. When Frederic entered, he rushed forward
and embraced him with real joy. Only then did he
remember that he had not yet saluted the mistress
of the house.

"I venture to hope that Madame de Marcoiran
will excuse my impoliteness," said he, bowing, in
some embarrassment, to the châtelaine.

"Upon one condition only, Messire Boucarut,"
said she, smiling. "Do you agree to it in advance?"

"I have too often imposed penances myself upon
others to refuse to perform my own."

"You promise?"

"Yes, Madame, counting upon your indulgence."

"Then I forgive you. Thérésine, set a cover at
table for Messire Boucarut. He will dine with us."

"No, dear Madame, I beg of you, not to-day;
you have company, and they are all strangers to me."

"You will make their acquaintance."

"Look at my dress—my old soutane."

"I will explain to my guests that if you have not
a new soutane, it is because you deprive yourself of
everything, spite of all that can be said or done, to
give to the poor."

"Oh, Madame, I beg of you, do not say that. It
would make me unhappy."

" You are too modest," said Frederic.

" No, my boy, only timid."

" The more reason that I cannot spare you, Messire," said Madame, " for you once told me yourself that some great saint declared timidity to be a touch of pride."

" It is true."

" So I must cure you of so terrible a vice," connued the noble lady.

" I submit to the first penance, but it is contrary to all canonical rules to impose a second for the same offence."

" Then, for this time, my mother will take pity on you, my excellent master, and refrain from mentioning your reason for wearing a garment which is not altogether new."

If she would also excuse me from being present—"

Even were I so disposed," said Madame, " it would be impossible. I hear our guests approaching now."

At that very moment the door opened, and the Marquis de Blésignan entered with his old friend the Commander.

" Messire Boucarut, curate of Notre Dame d'Amour," said Madame, presenting the ecclesiastic to them; then, turning to the priest: " The Marquis de Blésignan, Seigneur of Nyons, Blésignan, and other places, our honored kinsman. My brother the Commander."

The three men bowed and sat down.

"You inhabit a curious country, Messire," said the Marquis. "I never met its equal for originality."

"Poor but good," said the curate, nervously fingering his breviary and casting timid, furtive glances at the tall stranger with the rough voice, and nose hooked like a bird of prey, who fixed upon him a pair of greenish-gray eyes with phosphorescent lights in them, and showed, when he spoke, rows of close, white, pointed teeth, like those of a wolf.

The only thing in his hasty scrutiny which at all reassured him was that the Marquis seemed so careless about his own dress. A marquis who wears close-cropped hair, a large striped cravat, a long gray surtout, blue cashmere breeches, and long boots could not be very exacting about the costume of others.

To the trim undress uniform of the Queen's Dragoon and the scrupulously correct attire of the Commander, who wore a coat of Carmelite brown, a vest of the same color, striped breeches, buckled shoes, and a lace cravat wound several times round his neck, the costume of M. de. Blésignan offered a striking contrast.

But the priest had no anxiety as regarded them He knew he would meet with every indulgence from them, and the only thing which now alarmed him was the appearance of Mlle. de Blésignan, who Marius

had told him was a splendid young lady. She came
in wearing a simple white dress enlivened with ribbons, her hair curled in infantile fashion on her forehead and gathered in a rich mass at the back of her
head. None of those embroideries, jewels, or other
luxurious ornaments which had been so much in
vogue a few years before. She wore low-heeled
shoes, a simply-made, tight-fitting dress with open
sleeves.

Germaine, still more plainly dressed, had resumed
the Provençale garb in all its purity: a tight jacket,
or rather waist, of black velvet, with silver buttons;
a double muslin kerchief crossed on her breast; a
short skirt, falling in graceful folds. On her head,
surmounting the dark bands of hair brushed smoothly
on her forehead, was a high, pointed, white cap; it
was encircled by a broad black ribbon, edged with
narrow white lace, which fell in streamers over her
shoulders.

The poor priest, accustomed to the exaggerated
fashions which belonged to the early part of the
reign of Louis XVI.,—the paniers, the red heels, the
gigantic headgear, powdered, and surmounted by a
structure of feathers,—was astonished at so much
simplicity.

An optimist by temperament, and led by his own
virtue to be indulgent towards others, the worthy
curate was easily persuaded that all the changes which
had taken place since the coronation of Louis the

Just were so many steps towards the return of the
Golden Age; and what he now beheld with his own
eyes convinced him that the time was not far distant
when virtue alone would hold the sceptre in the
world.

Before she had spoken a word, Mlle. de Blésignan,
in whom he found a striking resemblance to one of
the angels, white-robed and golden-haired, in his
picture of the Assumption, had quite won the old
priest's heart.   He was really pleased to find himself
seated near her, especially when Germaine told him
that she had come all the way to Camargue on purpose to make a pilgrimage to the shrine of the three
Marys at les Saintes.

Whilst Madame, the Marquis, and the Commander
began to talk politics, the curate, avoiding that fiery
ground, took part in a much less stormy conversation
about the next day's pilgrimage.

"I know very well," said Renée to her cousin,
"that the Feast of the Marys is celebrated in Provence, in Languedoc, and other places besides.   I
have heard a good deal about it, yet I must admit
that I am not very well versed in the legend con-
nected with it, and really, before going to the tomb,
I would like to hear what relics it contains."

"The bones of the three Marys, Mademoiselle,"
said Frederic.

"The head of St. James and three of the heads of
the Holy Innocents," added Germaine.

" I know that much," said Renée; " but who are the three Marys themselves ? Neither the Blessed Virgin nor Mary Magdalen is among them. So I beg of you, Monsieur Frederic, to try and furbish up my somewhat rusty ideas."

" My own are a little confused, I must confess."

" Well, you, Germaine."

" There were Mary Jacobi and Mary Salome and Mary—oh, there I am lost."

" And Mary the mother of James," said Frederic.

" No, my dear Frederic," said Germaine, " Mary the mother of James, bishop of Jerusalem, is the same as Mary Jacobi."

" No, she cannot be."

" But I assure you I am right."

" Messire Boucarut will perhaps settle matters for us," said Renée, turning to the priest, " and kindly enlighten our ignorance."

" I shall esteem it a great honor to be useful to you in any way, Mademoiselle," said the priest, courteously.

" You can be both useful and agreeable to us all, Messire," said Renée, " if you will tell us something of the actual history of the three Marys."

" This legend is very simple," said the priest; " and since you wish to hear it, I will relate it just as the most accurate historians have handed it down to us.

" In the course of a violent persecution, instigated

by the high-priest Ananias, a few years after the
death of Our Saviour, the Jews seized numbers of
Christians and cast them into prison; but not daring
to put them to death, because there were many important personages among them, and, on the other
hand, fearing that the example of constancy given
by these courageous confessors might tend to increase
the number of the disciples of Christ, they resolved
to get rid of them in another way.

" They put them on board of a great vessel without sails, oars, or cordage, and towing them out into
the middle of the river, abandoned them to the fury
of the waves. Now in this vessel, amongst many
others of the faithful, were Mary the mother of
James, usually known as Mary Jacobi; Mary daughter of Salome; Marcella and Sarah, their servants;
Mary Magdalen; Martha, and Lazarus her brother;
Eutropius of Orange, George of Velay, Trophimius
of Arles, and many other saints, who became the first
apostles of Gaul.

" Having betaken themselves to prayer, God or-
dained that, gliding peacefully over the sea, the waves
whereof parted to give them passage, the wind should
blow them to that portion of the coast now the prov-
ince of Narbonne, where the Rhone falls into the sea,
surrounding the Stécades Isles."

" Pardon me, Messire, if I interrupt you," said
Renée, " but I must plead ignorance of all these
places."

" I should rather ask your pardon, noble lady,"
said the priest, " for not having given some explana-
tion of the names which occur in this legend. But
we are quite in our own neighborhood, for the Stécades Isles are really Provence and Camargue."

" Many thanks, Messire; will you now proceed
with your story ? "

" Having been thus miraculously delivered from
the perils of the sea," he resumed, " the holy travellers went down the shore to a short distance from
the Grau d'Orgon, and wishing to give thanks to
God, found a spot near at hand where there was a
little natural eminence. They erected an altar, constructed, for want of other materials, out of sand
and earth petrified by the waters of a spring which
God caused to gush forth in answer to their
prayers."

" These miracles were no doubt the origin of the
church of les Saintes ? " asked Renée.

" Yes, in this sense, that they determined these illustrious exiles to convert the place into an oratory
dedicated to God, in honor of the Blessed Virgin;
after which, leaving their companions to go forth
over the whole country bringing the light of Christianity everywhere, the holy Marys, Mary Magdalen,
Mary Jacobi, and Salome, with their followers, resolved to settle in that place. They had a cell built
adjoining the oratory, where they passed the rest of
their lives in the practice of the most sublime virtues."

" Does the present church date back to that remote period ? "

" It is fortunate that my uncle is quite absorbed
in his discussion on the future States-General," said
Frederic in a low voice to Renée.

" Why is it fortunate ? " asked she.

" Because he would forthwith begin upon history,
ancient stones, medals, and Heaven knows what besides.   And, if he had heard your question, he would
prove by an endless dissertation that if the ancient
church were not built in the first century, it must
have been built in the second, third, fourth, or fifth,
at least that it was neither in the tenth nor the elev-
enth, and that if the Emperor Constantine was not
the architect thereof, it was Guillaume de Provence,
or Count Bertrand, or some other, for the church
was really not built by any one person."

" You are cruel to learned men," said Renée.

" I am not afraid of pistols or swords in a hand-to-
hand combat," said Frederic, " but I do fear stones,
and Latin even more."

" Yet it is a noble language, and the language of
the Church."

" Do you know it ? "

" No, I regret to say I do not."

" I am glad to hear that you do not," said Germaine, " for, according to one of our proverbs, there
is nothing so dangerous for a woman."

" I never heard of such a proverb," said Renée.

"Well, here it is :

> ' Fiho que mounto, vacco que descend
> Capélan que danso, fumo que parlo latin,
> Au toujours fa marido fin.'"*

"Unhappily for me, my dear Germaine," said Renée, "I do not know Provençale any better than Latin."

"That is a pity in our Camargue," said Germaine, proceeding to translate the proverb for her.

"Yet you must remember," said Renée, laughing, "that in the archives of our convent were preserved, as a great honor to the community, some Latin verses composed in honor of Notre Dame de Rochefort by a religious of St. Praxeda named Julienne Morel."

"She probably died young and met with a violent death," said Frederic, "for there would not be a just Providence if she did not suffer an exemplary punishment proportioned to her crime."

"She died quietly in her bed, at the age of eighty," said Renée, "in spite of the aggravating circumstance that she spoke twelve foreign languages."

"If she had confined herself to one she would be alive yet," said the Dragoon, coolly.

"And meanwhile I have not yet heard the history of the church whither we are going to-morrow."

---

* "A girl who ascends from the plain to the mountain,
A cow which thence descends,
A priest who dances, a woman who speaks Latin,
Will all come to a bad end."

" This church," said the priest, " is just behind the oratory, and it was built under the following circumstances.   Of the altar of clay erected by the first apostles of Provence, and of the marble slab put up to their memory by the faithful immediately after their death, only some remnants are preserved.   The oratory and grove were but a heap of ruins when a poor hermit came to establish himself there, where the Saracens had destroyed everything.   This was about the end of the tenth century, when a king of Arles, who, according to the chronicle, was devoted to the pleasures of the chase, and on that account frequented the forests of Camargue, met one day with the hermit, who told him that the bodies of the holy women were buried in that neighborhood.   The king immediately gave orders that the ruins should be inclosed by an edifice which was at once a church and a fortress."

" A church I can understand," said Renée, " but why a fortress ? "

" On account of the Saracens or Moors, Mademoiselle."

" Did they venture to advance that far at so late a period ? " said Renée.

" Alas ! Mademoiselle, even in the last century, that is to say, less than a hundred years ago, their vessels appeared so frequently upon these shores that the inhabitants of Aigues-Mortes addressed a petition to the king, Francis I., begging him to provide them with some means of combating these abominable infidels, who by armed force took away from the very gates of the town the women and children employed in the salt-works, taking them to Algeria, where they sold them as slaves."

" Why, even in our own day," said Frederic, " spite of the lesson given them by Louis XIV., these pirates had the insolence to cruise about the very entrance to the port of Marseilles, and to seize upon fishing-boats or even trading-vessels, which they rob, and the crews of which they take into that cursed country whence the Fathers of Mercy are ransoming captives every year."

" A day will come," cried the priest, " when our kings will put an end to this piracy, by invading these wretches in their haunts. To the eldest daughter of the Church, and to her glorious monarch, who, on ascending the throne of France, has sought to dispel every trace of bondage, belongs the accomplishment of this last act of justice, an act to be enrolled in that book of honor on the first page of which is written, 'Gesta Dei per Francos,' the Works of God by the French."

" Be happy, Mlle. de Blésignan," murmured Frederic; " there is Latin for you now."

" And beautiful Latin," said the young girl, in a voice quivering with emotion; " it is the bead-roll of honor for our nation."

The priest modestly resumed.

" From that time forth the faithful were enabled
to proceed, as before, to the long-deserted shrine.
Many miracles were wrought there; and the number
of pilgrims ever increasing, in course of time a little
to wn grew up which was also surrounded by fortified
walls, and bore successively the names of Notre
Dame de la Barque, de la Mer, and at last des Saintes
Maries. This state of things might have lasted for
centuries, had not good King René of Anjou come
thither, to venerate the sacred relics. He then
learned that these relics, the presence of which was
attested by numberless miracles, were still buried
under heaps of rubbish, and that their exact vicinity
was unknown. From the researches instituted by
the pious monarch and carried on with equal ardor
and intelligence, the oratory, altar, and grotto were
each disclosed in turn; and at last the relics of the
three Marys, the head of St. James and those of the
Innocents, brought from the East by the holy women.
The relics thus collected, enclosed in costly reliqua-
ries, were publicly exposed in the church, which was
considerably enlarged and solemnly consecrated, in
presence of the kings of Provence and Bavaria, accompanied by three or four hundred lords, the Cardinal Legate of the Holy See, twelve bishops, and
a host of other ecclesiastics, not to mention an immense multitude of people, on the third December,
1448.

" So, noble lady, that is all I can tell you about

the church and the precious relics that you will have
the happiness of visiting to-morrow."

"*Cornebleu!*" vociferated the Marquis, rapping
on the table with the handle of his knife, "it makes
my blood boil to hear of these States-General and
these Parliaments, a set of brawlers and blockheads.
And alone against them all His Majesty the King
of France, whom they seek to thwart in every con-
ceivable way. But he has not acted once as he
should have done. I mean going in to their con-
claves, booted, spurred, and whip in hand."

" All historians do not agree in thinking such conduct praiseworthy on the part of a king; for after all,
Monsieur, after all, my dear Marquis, parliamentary
government is—"

" A government of blockheads!" cried the Marquis, " a government of attorneys, lawyers, money-
grabbers, and dice-players. Instead of disputing with
such scoundrels, who have done more harm to the
Kingdom of the Lilies than the swarms of locusts do
to your Camargue, His Majesty should have said to
them, once for all: ' I am the State.' "

" Still," objected the Commander, passing his hand
through the artistically-arranged ringlets of his short
white wig, " history tells us—"

" History tells us," interrupted the irascible gentleman, " that when France was in danger Louis
XIV. said: ' I and my nobility will mount our horses,
and save the kingdom.' And he did save it, as he

had promised, sword in hand and spur on heel, which would not have been the case, if instead of his nobility, whose blood has dyed the banners of France, he had appealed to those babblers in spectacles, with their big portfolios, who can only fight with the tongue or ride on benches."

"Our good and venerated sovereign does not see things as you do, my dear Marquis," said Madame, gently; "in his opinion the title of Father of the People is above all others, and, that he may the better know the wants and wishes of his children, he seeks light from the representatives of the three orders."

"This light, Madame, is an incendiary torch; nothing else. France does not gain by it, and the king will lose his crown. Remember what I tell you. Charles I. of England had the best intentions; he confided in his Parliament, and placed his power in their hands. What happened? When the king was nothing, the Parliament, his dear Parliament, was everything, and took the opportunity to cut off the king's head."

"It is to be hoped that the future States-General will not go as far as that."

"*Cornebleu!* I do not know about that. You say, hope; I say, prevent: it is the more prudent plan."

"As we have finished, we may as well go into the drawing-room for our coffee," said Madame, who feared that the discussion was growing too warm.

Though very excitable, M. de Blésignan was none the less a well-bred man. He rose at once, and offered his hand to Madame, whom he gallantly escorted to her place in the drawing-room, excusing himself, as they went, for his too great warmth.

Unfortunately, it was not only at the *Château Rouge* that the acts of the government were discussed with acrimony: now it was the somewhat feeble and hesitating policy of Louis XVI., or again the bitterness with which the opponents of royalty tore not only the ministry but the King and Queen to pieces. Against these victims of a future revolution arose from every side a storm of squibs, libels, caricatures, and calumnious pamphlets.

" It began with songs, but will end with cannon," said Beaumarchais.

This was in 1788, and Louis XVI. had been already fourteen years upon the throne. He had not desired royalty. A secret presentiment had seemed to warn him that power was an abyss which was to engulf him. Marie-Antoinette, his wife, the daughter of the immortal Empress Maria Theresa, also dreaded it.

When in 1774 news was brought to this couple, born for good but predestined to suffering and misfortune, of the death of Louis XV., they both fell on their knees, crying out:

" My God, protect us, direct us: we are too young."

The reign of the new sovereign was inaugurated by a series of benefits to the people. Within a few years Louis had established in Paris the Mont-de-Piété * and a *caisse d'escompte* † which prevented all danger of a panic; secured the payment of the municipal taxes; replaced the *corvée* or contribution in forced labor of the feudal times by a pecuniary stipend; abolished in Franche-Comté the last remnants of territorial servitude; erased from the civil code such traces of barbarism as the previous question and the torture; renounced the onerous right of the *joyeux avénement ;*‡ re-established the Parliaments which the nation demanded; called into power the men chosen by public opinion; and aided America in its struggle against England.   What more could he do ?

So much did he love his people, whom he called his lambs, that when, during a severe winter, the courtiers begged him to try sleighing as an amusement, he replied: " Those are the only sleighs which please me," pointing, as he spoke, to the heavy carts loaded with wood bought with his own money, to be distributed among the poor.

It was this same king who said to his ministers, when urged to sign a warrant for the punishment of the mutineers: " Let us begin, gentlemen, by exam-

---

* The famous loan-bank in Paris for the relief of the people.
† Discount-bank.
‡ Besides the ordinary seignorial payments, the king was entitled, on his accession, to the right of *joyeux avénement*, for confirming in their appointments all officers depending directly on the crown.

ining our own conduct, to see whether in these sad events there has not been some fault on our side."

Marie-Antoinette, by her exquisite kindliness, proved herself worthy of the King. On her arrival in France, her beauty had won all hearts; a charming saying of hers had preceded her at the court and prepossessed every one in her favor. Her royal mother once asked her over which country she would prefer to reign. "Over France," she answered, "which was governed by Henri IV. and Louis XIV.; for the example of the one teaches us the beautiful, and that of the other the good."

As Louis XVI. had renounced the right of the *joyeux avénement*, so the Queen renounced that of the *ceinture*.* She had a share in all his charities, and gave such abundant alms that the poor, whom she had assisted with an exquisite grace and unwearying benevolence, raised to her in the Rue St. Honoré, during a severe winter, a pyramid of snow bearing this inscription, composed by some contemporary writer:

"Reine dont la beauté surpassé les appas,
    Près d'un roi biènfaisant occupe ici la place;
Si ce monument frêle est de neige et de glace,
    Nos cœurs pour toi ne le sont pas." †

* Queen's Girdle, a tax imposed upon all goods which came into Paris by the Seine.
† "Queen whose beauties surpass all charms,
    Occupying a place here beside a gen'rous king,
If this frail monument be of snow and ice,
    Such are not our hearts towards thee."

But the veneration of the people for these sovereigns quickly passed away, and respect was changed to ridicule. Voltaire, who was still living, had taught the new generation to mock at and to drag in the mire all that had once been sacred in France. The revolutionary spirit, which proceeds as naturally from atheistical philosophy as death from the poison of a venomous snake, combined with the criminal levity and thoughtless frivolity of certain pamphleteers to discredit the government. They began by singing songs against the King and Queen, and to songs and caricatures succeeded the vilest calumnies. Bred in a court noted for its simplicity, Marie-Antoinette, on coming to France, was at first opposed to all tedious formalities, and made her own beauty her sole adornment. This did not satisfy a court accustomed to luxury and extravagance. A celebrated jeweler was sent to her, who deplored the decline of his trade in France; in her simplicity, the young Queen fell into the snare and bought diamonds from him. Then came manufacturers from Lyons with all their various stuffs. She thought herself obliged to wear sumptuous garments. The pamphlets at once took up the hue and cry, and exclaimed with feigned indignation that *l'Autrichienne* (the Austrian) was insulting the public misery and ruining France. They declared that she had created a new ministry in France, in favor of Madame Bertin, her dressmaker. These false accusations drew the first tears from the young Queen's eyes. She had arrayed herself thus merely through kindness of heart. In 1794 she sold her diamonds to purchase wheat for the poor, appeared everywhere in the most simple costumes, and a wheel of her carriage having come off as she was driving to the opera, she took an ordinary cab and continued her way.

Immediately there was an outcry upon her neglect of decorum and contempt for etiquette; the Queen, it was declared, by acting thus had set her ladies an example of bad taste, and the balladists published these insolent verses, which were affixed to walls in the most public places:

> " Petite reine de vingt ans,
> Vous qui traitez si mal les gens,
> Vous repasserez la barrière," etc.*

Matters grew worse when, disgusted with the courtiers who, under a semblance of false respect, spied upon her actions to turn her into ridicule, she tried to create for herself an intimate circle where she might be loved and appreciated for herself alone.

Ridicule was then succeeded by the most cowardly calumnies; libels were circulated reflecting upon her character; the famous affair of the necklace, which was associated with the name of the Queen, who had no knowledge whatever of the matter, obtained a deplorable notoriety. The most innocent amuse-

---

* " Little queen of twenty years,
  You who treat so badly your peers,
  You will be sent over the frontiers," etc.

ments of this unfortunate princess were made an
occasion for scandal.

Tired of the splendors of Versailles, she loved to
retire to Trianon, a pavilion close by the park, of
which Louis had made her a present.

There, free at last, clad in a gown of white percale,
with a gauze kerchief and a simple straw hat, she
loved to watch the milking of the cows, or to fish in
the lake, in company with the Princess de Lamballe
and the Countess de Polignac. Surely there could
be no more innocent amusement. Yet it was sufficient to raise the cry that the abomination of desolation had come. The Austrian had hidden herself
there to plot against France; the groves and the pavilion were said to be the scene of the most abominable orgies, and so on.

Poor Queen! Providence prepared her for martyrdom by suffering.

Nor was the King more fortunate. Every act of
his was made a reproach against him. He only desired the happiness of his subjects; he was simple,
generous, inspired by the purest motives. It seemed
to be his destiny that his best actions should be
represented as crimes, and he had reason to feel the
cruel truth uttered by the virtuous Malesherbes:

"That extreme sensibility, that tender humanity,
and all the qualities which ordinarily make the best
kings, become in times of revolution as bad as, and
in their consequences even more fatal than, vices."

France seemed seized with a vertigo. The Revolution, which was the outcome of disorder and impiety, was advancing with giant strides before those who were to be its first victims had heard the first rumblings of the storm. Moreover, many nobles, merchants, and even some priests, carried away by love of novelty, indifference, apathy, or that they might not run any risk, favored its progress, and considered as obstinate or violent the more farseeing men who would have combated it energetically from the beginning.

Such was the state of France in 1788.

CHAPTER V.

THE PILGRIMAGE.

THAT evening they all separated early, for M. de Forton prudently reminded them that if they would avoid the burning heat of the day they must set out at dawn, or, to make use of his own more poetic expression borrowed from Fénelon and the poets of the golden age, " before the dawn with rosy fingers opened the gates of the east to the horses of Phœbus."

Thanks to this precaution, they were all ready when, at half-past three in the morning, Marius came to inform the gentlemen, and Thérésine the ladies, that the horses and the carriage were waiting in the court. In a quarter of an hour Jean-de-Dieu cracked his whip as a signal of departure for the whole caravan.

Wrapped in a hooded cloak like that of Germaine, Renée led the way between Frederic and Germaine, mounted on those small horses peculiar to the country, with the massive head but delicate and nervous legs. They .·e as gentle as indefatigable. They grow up unrestrained in the open air. They are the direct descendants of the Arab horses brought into

Camargue by the Saracens. Just behind this advance-guard came the carriage, containing Madame, the Marquis de Blésignan, and the Abbé Boucarut. The latter, absorbed in reciting his breviary, left his impetuous neighbor, who was happily somewhat calmed after his night's rest, to prelude by an agricultural dissertation with the Commander, still faithful to his rôle of attendant squire, a stormy discussion upon political questions.

A cariole with three horses brought all the house people except Bernard, who was kept at home by his rheumatism. This was under the special guidance of Thérésine, who, having given up her pony to Renée, confined herself to the humble but useful occupation of driver. She also kept an eye upon the provisions which, with her usual happy forethought, she had packed in large *canastelles* (baskets).

Gun on shoulder, and a colored handkerchief tied carelessly around his neck, Marius followed with half a dozen guardians armed with spears and proceeding in picturesque disorder.

The weather was splendid but cold; some light fleecy clouds floated through the heavens, growing tinged with rose as they approached that point upon the horizon where, unfolding gradually before the still invisible sun, was the mantle of purple, fringed with gold, which the morn spreads beneath his feet.

On the Valcarès side—for the cavalcade pursued its way along its reed-crowned banks—a thick gray mist rolled softly up from the dull and sleeping waters; that is to say, on the other side, over all the plain, glided rather than floated a half-transparent haze, while the dew embroidered the reeds and rushes with pearls fallen from the jewel-case of the night. These pearly drops likewise attached themselves to the clothing or to the beards of our travellers, no less than to the manes of their horses.

The pilgrims had taken various precautions to counteract the injurious effects of this mist which always precedes the sun. They had each drunk a cup of black coffee or a small glass of brandy before setting out, and were provided with thick cloaks. Besides, all except the guardians, who were long accustomed to breathe these malarial vapors, drew a corner of their cloak over their mouth.

Warned in advance by her friend, Mlle. de Blésignan imitated her companion, and, half veiling her face like the Arab woman, contented herself with observing the singular effects produced by the rising sun on this landscape half effaced by the mist. The mist, far from being dispelled, grew thicker and thicker as the eastern sky became redder and redder.

The profound silence which reigned over the plain heightened the effect of this scene, to which the very vagueness of the objects lent a certain weirdness.

From time to time the neighing of a horse, or the rustle of the bulrushes, from amongst which a wild duck, frightened by the unexpected approach of the horses, fled with a great flapping of wings, alone broke in upon the stillness.

The eye had no more occupation than the ear. The habitations were sparsely scattered along the banks of the Valcarès; sometimes they were merely cabins, appearing ever and anon dimly through the mist, or vanishing in its greater thickness; the day itself had a sort of twilight look, something weird and unreal.

All at once a great light burst upon the landscape, and the sun appeared like a vast globe of fire, not now on the mountain-heights, but close to the ground, spreading a golden veil over the whole plain at once, and sending afar the shadows of the riders, unnaturally elongated. Never had Renée seen such a sunrise: it filled her with amazement. The wand of a magician could have produced nothing rarer or more magical than this sudden awakening of nature; the whole landscape was illumined at once; the mist turned from gray to brilliant white, and seemed to shrink as if compressed by a superior force.

Yet it grew denser and more dense, the ground, as far as eye could reach, was apparently covered with snow; above and beyond the mist the air was of an extreme purity and of almost incredible transparency. Above it was summer, below it was winter. The struggle did not last long; the artificial snow vanished in the sand; it resisted longer over the water; but at last the sun triumphed; the remnant of the thick veil, rent into a thousand pieces, hung here and there

over the stream upon its crown of reeds, forming as
it were an irregularly-carved frame to the waters,
which had become all at once blue and sparkling.
Then, under the ardor of its rays, the whole mist was
condensed into drops, which, each reflecting the light,
changed into precious stones, emeralds, diamonds,
sapphires, or rubies, glittering out from among the
verdure.   It was a general illumination.

All nature awoke at the same moment.   In an
instant the air was full of joyous sounds: the neighing
of horses saluting the rising of the sun; the lowing of
the bulls lying here and there along the *roubine;* the
tinkling of cow-bells; the hoarse notes of the guardians' call; the silvery trilling of the lark borne on the
morning breeze; the shrill whistle of the water-
fowl in the marshes, and the distant bellowing of the
herds.   Earth, air, and water seemed peopled as if by
enchantment; flocks of ducks plunged into the lake,
the surface of which was already disturbed by the
dipping of the wings of black swallows and white gulls;
the partridges ran about in the plain, whence flew
flamingoes and herons, dislodged from the sedges by
troops of cattle with tapering horns; on the distant
horizon galloped, with tail and mane in the breeze,
herds of young horses, that, evidently distrustful,
sniffed the air and pursued their mad course, raising a
cloud of dust; the heaven was full of birds, the air of
mosquitoes: clouds of locusts arose out of the sand
under the horses' feet.

' Now we may throw aside our cloaks and converse at our ease," said Germaine, throwing off her hood. Renée asked nothing better: there were so many wonderful things to see. They came just then to the cabin of the Masques, close to a vast bank of reeds, the greenness of which contrasted well with the snowy whiteness of the Sansouire; twenty or thirty bulls were carelessly stretched upon the ground or browsing peaceably, in the marsh close to the shore. On the approach of the horses they raised their heads, and one of them advanced, bellowing. Mlle. de Blésignan, who was not accustomed to such encounters, felt the presence of this black bulk more than alarming.

"Is it safe to pass them?" she said, looking at Frederic.

Germaine laughed, and, urging her pony to a gallop, made straight at the threatening beast, which seemed as if barring the passage.

"My God!" cried Renée, turning pale, "Germaine will be hurt."

But there was no reason to fear. Intimidated by the approach of the intrepid rider, the bull turned away, and trotted heavily back into the marsh.

"You see there is not so much danger," said Germaine, returning; "our bulls when in troops never attack, and will hardly defend themselves. The only danger is when one meets a single bull escaped from the herd. Solitude makes them fierce; fortunately that does not often happen, only when

the bulls are changing pasture and one is left be·
hind.   Even in that case he is usually very quickly
found."

"To find him would be one thing," said Renée,
"and to bring him back another."

"There is nothing easier," said Frederic.   "Do
you see? yonder a guardian is galloping about with
his spear."

"I see him very well; I thought the bull was
chasing him."

"*Following* him is the more correct expression.
That bull, as you call him, is a tamed ox, who has
become a tamer, or *dondaire*, as they express it here,
in his turn.   He wears a bell on his neck.   If one of
the herd strays, the guardian goes after him, accompanied by this tamer, the tinkling of whose bell
suffices to bring back the most wicked and undis-
ciplined bull to a sense of duty.   No sooner does the
sound of the bell fall upon the ear of the fugitive
than he hastens to place himself beside the *dondaire*,
and is brought back by him without making the least
resistance."

"But suppose he took it into his head to make
some resistance?" asked Renée, doubtfully.

"The guardian would punish him with his spear,
and if necessary the tamed bull would let him feel the
point of his horns.   Sometimes, however, the guardian disdains this useful auxiliary, and, anxious to
make a name among his comrades, confronts the bull

alone, struggles with him, throws him down, and then brings him back, abashed and humiliated, to his herd."

"A man fight a bull and bring him back alone!" cried Renée. "Ah, in spite of all the extraordinary things I have seen here, I believe that in this matter you are imposing upon my credulity."

"Not in the least, my dear," said Germaine; "and perhaps in a day or two I may be able to show you not one but several duels of this sort, and you shall see that of the two adversaries the man is always the stronger and more adroit."

"What sort of men are these guardians?"

"You have already made the acquaintance of some of them," said Germaine. "Marius, our overseer, was a guardian for several years. Only, they must be trained to the work young; they must train their bodies till they are steeled against fatigue, hunger, and cold; they must avoid all intemperance, and their souls must be devoid of all fear. On these conditions they become kings of Camargue, for, though we inhabit it, the bull-drivers are really its masters; their sceptre is the trident of iron; their palace a canvas tent, wherein they sleep on the bare ground; their throne a wild horse; their crown a handkerchief knotted around their forehead; their royal mantle a blouse of leather or sheepskin; their subjects the black herd, which tremble before them, obey their voices, and rush after them like an avalanche when they give the shrill signal of departure and urge their ponies to a gallop, or stop at once when commanded."

Conversing thus, Germaine, who was the improvised guide of the expedition, was still following the river road, when Marius came galloping up to the head of the caravan.

"The Commander sent me to tell you to turn to the right," said he, addressing Germaine; "the water is high, and the carriage can never pass through the rice-plantations of Frignan."

"Are you sure?" asked Frederic.

"Perfectly sure, Monsieur; Espérit, the guardian from Sylveréal, who crossed there yesterday evening, declares that even on horseback one can scarcely pass through it."

"That is really too bad," said Frederic, "for midway there I intended to show you some antiquities which, I am sure, would have interested you very much."

"There are antiquities here, then?"

"Yes, Roman ruins, half submerged now by the stream, which has grown considerably since that epoch."

"So the Romans came into this country?"

"Yes, they not only came, but settled here for some time; it is to them, if we may credit a learned dissertation of my uncle the Commander's, that our island owes its name of Camargue."

"I would never have supposed so."

"And yet it is certain, always accepting the authority of my honored uncle, for I never take the responsibility of these assertions even though they be supported by academicians and other learned people on our customs or derivation."

"Give me your etymology; you know I have a weakness for Latin."

"Well, here it is. A certain Marius, a Roman general, came, no one knows precisely why or wherefore, to spend some time among the marshes with a legion, who soon—but that is easily understood—got tired of the place, and mutinied to be taken away from it; but Caius Marius, who treated his soldiers much as the guardians treat their bulls, irritated by the insubordination of his legion, determined to punish their rebellion. Instead of acceding to their demands he set them to dig ditches, to remove the sand, to open canals. In this way he turned the whole region topsy-turvy; so that the island, which had been theretofore known as the Stécade, took the name of the field of Caius Marius, in Latin *Caii Marii ager*, in French *Camargue*."

"So you see Latin is useful sometimes."

"Oh, so seldom!"

"In this case it gives us a very curious etymology."

"I would rather it pointed out the way we should take just now, for I see that my sister is as much puzzled as I am."

"If Monsieur wishes," said Marius, "I will send

Truphême to lead the way as far as the pasture of la Trinité, from which we can see the *Mas Brun*."

"Yes, send him, or we shall never get on."

Marius rode back and sent one of the guardians forward. He was a fresh-complexioned, sun-burned lad, who managed his half-wild horse like a centaur, and galloped on in advance of the caravan.

"Do you know the road well?" asked Germaine as this individual passed her.

The guardian replied by a laugh which was more like a growl, and, pointing to a distant speck upon the horizon, which his eyes alone could discover, set off at once.

In less than an hour after they were at the *Mas*, where they stopped a few minutes to let their horses take breath. From this time forward their way was clear; they followed the road from Arles to les Saintes, which was bordered by a sinuous line of trees, accompanying the capricious windings of the second branch of the Rhone, just before the spot where it throws itself into the sea, close by the Saintes-Maries.

"Are you not fatigued, my dear," inquired Madame of Renée, "between the heat and the mosquitoes?"

"Really, Madame, I never even thought of them," said Renée; "my eyes are so busy and so delighted with all that they see."

"Would you not rather get into the carriage for the rest of the journey?"

among the graves, and is much affected by beggars, cripples, and the infirm of all kinds, who come from great distances, not so much to pray for their cure as to excite the compassion of charitable souls. There they sleep in the open air, there they eat and drink. The gravestones serve them alternately as tables or pillows.

This strange assembly is composed not only of beggars and cripples: pickpockets and dice-players mingle there with gypsies, of whom the tawdry women and half-naked children grovel in this stronghold of misery and vice; toothless hags, fortune-tellers with blear eyes and parchment skin, also congregate there; it is, in fact, a little world of thieves and beggars, who find in the pilgrimage an opportunity of plying their trade. Such young and distinguished visitors could not fail to excite their greed. They were quickly surrounded by beggars, some extending their hands and whining, others displaying their sores; they were fairly besieged by ragged children clinging to their garments, and intimidated neither by the cane of the Marquis nor the whip of the young officer. The coins distributed by the young ladies only added to the confusion. Renée was frightened, and would fain have got back to the gate; but the circle of repulsive faces seemed to close in about her. The two gentlemen had to open a passage for her by force. They were almost at the gate, when a hideous old hag, seizing Renée's hand, whispered in her ear:

"Noble lady, be generous to poor Deborah, and she will tell you your fortune."

"Let me alone," said Renée, shuddering at her touch; "I do not want any lying predictions that proceed from the devil."

But, instead of letting go, the hag passed her bony finger over the palm of Renée's hand.

"You will wed a handsome gentleman, my darling," said she; "a brilliant officer, who—"

"Go away, you ugly creature!" said Renée, trying to draw away her hand, and frightened when she could not succeed in wresting it from the old woman's grasp.

"Begone, you old witch!" said Frederic, pushing the crone aside, so hastily that she fell into a new-made grave.

"Hearken, noble lady," cried the hag, furiously shaking her fist, "you will wed, not this officer, but Death himself upon the scaffold; and he, too, will come to a violent end."

The Queen's Dragoon did not hear these threats, but they pierced Renée's heart like a dagger.

"It was wrong of me to bring you here," said Germaine, seeing how pale her friend looked. "Are you ill?"

"No, dear friend," said Renée, "and I am not usually so easily impressed. I am really ashamed of my ridiculous fright, which has now passed off."

Germaine would no doubt have insisted, but at this

moment the bell rang for the last time, and she saw her mother and the Commander, with the prior, who invited them to enter, and offered them holy water.

Fortunately there were new emotions and new surprises to divert Renée's mind from the scene in the cemetery. Profoundly Christian, and full of tender and ardent piety, she could not remain unmoved by a spectacle which touched even the coldest natures. Nothing could be plainer, we might almost say more bare, than the church of les Saintes. It had only a single nave, inflanked by chapels formed by Roman arches of a most severe style, and adorned with humble *ex-votos*. One of the chapels marks the spot where once stood the oratory of the Marys, of which nothing remains but a fountain, or rather a well, almost close to the ground; near which the Abbé Boucarut, in surplice and stole, stood offering to the faithful a cup of water from the miraculous spring, which they drank, crossing themselves, and laid a modest offering on the plate placed beside the well.

A few wooden steps led from the aisle to the chancel, between the double balustrade of which could be seen the dome of the crypt; above this was a semicircular apsis, forming a flat surface, decorated with many lights and prepared for the exposition of the relics. Just opposite this, in the background, was the seigneurial pew, beside the altar, and under the upper chapel where the relics are kept. Usually the whole place is cold, bare, deserted; but then,

from the pew, Renée saw before and beneath her a
dense multitude, so closely packed that their heads
seemed to touch, and a whole forest of lighted tapers.
It resembled a grain-field of which every ear was a
flame. A profound silence had succeeded to the
previous tumult; they awaited the coming of the
Saints; all eyes were fixed upon the upper window,
at which the relics, the object of all their hopes, were
to appear. The altar was resplendent; incense
floated upwards in long spiral curves towards the
roof, where it was lost in a thick cloud; every heart
was oppressed, every breast heaved; in the silence
the whisper of many prayers could be heard, or ever
and anon a sigh which proceeded from the holy impatience, inspired by faith, of a sick person who had
come to pray for his cure. There was something
indescribably solemn in this moment of suspense.

All at once the window was thrown open, and the
reliquary was first placed upon the sill, and then
raised by a pulley, and let down slowly into the void,
with a scarcely-perceptible movement. Supplicating
hands were upraised in all directions; there was an
outburst of prayers, supplications, cries, and tears:

"Holy Marys, pray for us! Holy Marys, cure
my child! Holy Marys, be propitious to us!"

And with an indescribable manifestation of faith
all arms were outstretched, and there was a general
rush towards that ark of salvation which it sufficed to
touch in order to obtain a cure.

Renée heard no more. Bathed in tears, her head buried in her hands, amid the storm of hymns which shook the roof, and the storm of supplications which went up around her, she repeated :

"Servants of God, great Saint Marys, enlighten me upon my vocation; give me strength to imitate you, and obtain for me the favor that my father may consent to let me, too, consecrate myself to the service of God."

She prayed long and fervently. When, at length, she raised her head, she found herself alone with Madame, who said :

"It is time to go, my dear."

"Already?" cried she.

"It is late; the others are waiting for us at the priory."

As Renée still hesitated, Madame said :

"The relics will remain exposed for twenty-four hours; if you like, we will come back, my child."

"How good you are, mother!" said Renée, pressing her hand.

Madame's face brightened.

"The saints must have worked a miracle in our favor," thought she; "her father will be delighted, and so shall we."

CHAPTER VI.

RENÉE.

RENÉE had been deeply touched by the wonderful scene she had just witnessed. When
she entered the priory, Germaine remarked that her
eyes were red with weeping; but, out of delicacy, she
appeared not to notice, and, seeing her sad and
thoughtful, proposed for her benefit a walk through
the town. Renée would have refused; but as all the
rest, including Madame de Marcoiran, seemed disposed to go, she felt bound to acquiesce.

At that time, as the offices of the day were over,
and those of the night not to commence for some
hours, the idle crowd had dispersed noisily through
the streets or on the square, where booths, lit up by
tallow candles, displayed their treasures to the won-
der-stricken eyes of the wives and daughters of guardians or salt-workers.

Swarms of peasant women buzzed and hummed,
and waved their broad ribbons round the stalls filled
with tapers, statues, beads, and pictures. The young
men, a coat thrown over one shoulder, a colored

handkerchief knotted around the neck, sat about the taverns, or surrounded the tent, under which, to the discordant music of flutes and tambourines, wooden horses were turned.

Around the walls the spectacle was still more picturesque. From the obscurity shone out bivouac-fires, embroidering the mantle of night with their luminous darts, and casting their red glare upon groups of fishermen and gypsies, whose attitudes, grouping, and picturesque costume seemed to await the pencil of Callot.* Renée had seen some of these dark children of Egypt from time to time, but she had never met with such multitudes of them, or in such garb. She remarked this to her friend.

"They come here in great numbers every year," said Germaine; "but this time Rebecca, the Queen of Egypt, being dead, they have collected in unusual force to give her a successor."

"Why here more than anywhere else?"

"Because," laughed Frederic, "les Saintes is the Rheims where these black sovereigns cause themselves to be consecrated."

"Have they, then, any sort of a temple or Mecca here?" asked Renée, whose curiosity was excited.

---

* Jacques Callot, an artist of Lorraine, who died in 1635, was specially distinguished for his sketches of gypsy life. He ran away from his father's house, and lived for a time among these bohemians, simply to study their costumes, manners, etc. He etched according to a process of his own, and has left many more engravings than paintings.

" Their Mecca is our church, my dear," said Germaine.

" What, they are Christians?"

" Not at all."

" Yet they are allowed into the church?"

" Not into the church proper," interrupted the Commander, " but into the crypt or subterranean church, under the chancel, where we were, and which is reserved for Saint Sarah, the servant of the holy women, and, according to tradition, an Egyptian by birth."

" I should like very much to be present at their pilgrimage," said Renée; " they must have a singular way of honoring their patron."

" Unfortunately the election of the queen took place at the same time as the descent of the relics," said Germaine. " But no matter; there may be a good many of the more devout gypsies in the crypt still, and, if you like, my brother and I will take you down there."

" And I will be delighted to make one of the party," said the Commander, bowing low.

I will be highly honored, Monsieur," said Renée, ` if we are not imposing on your good-nature and interrupting your walk."

" The honor will be mine, Mademoiselle, and I know my sister begins to find the air too cool and the mosquitoes too importunate, so that she is anxious to go in."

"Will not you join us, Monsieur le Marquis?" inquired Germaine.

"With your permission and Madame de Marcoiran's leave," said the Marquis, "I will return with her to the priory, where I shall find her interesting conversation much more agreeable than the sight of ragged gypsies and the unpleasant odor they exhale."

The priory was quite close to the church, and the company, leaving the shore, upon which the solemn murmur of the waves was heard, went up into the square. A little door opened upon a spiral staircase on the exterior of the chancel, giving access to both the church and crypt. Before going down M. de Forton removed his two watches and his snuffbox, and prudently placed them in an inner pocket. Whilst the Commander was finishing his preparations half a dozen Egyptians arrived, each bearing a taper decorated with ribbons and tinsel, and of an unusual thickness. Their chief wore a large felt hat trimmed with ribbons, wide black velvet Mameluke trousers, and a broad red sash round his waist, in which was stuck a huge pair of shears such as these nomads use to crop their mules, and sometimes to fight.

His companions, strong, dark-skinned fellows with black woolly hair, were the real brigands of the melodrama, clad in ragged velvet, with rings on their fingers, earrings in their ears, breastpins, and large buttons of carved silver on coat or waistcoat, and were of no more reassuring aspect than the first.

" I would rather," whispered Renée to Germaine, " meet these blackamoors, with their white teeth and sparkling eyes, in a church than in a forest."

" Hum ! " said M. de Forton, who had just finished taking an inventory of his valuables, " I would not advise you to depend too much on these rascals' respect for the sanctity of the place. To rob a Catholic is an act of piety for them."

" If a sculptor desired to make a statue of Prudence, I should suggest my uncle as a model," whispered Frederic, offering his arm to Renée, to lead her down the dark stairs. When they had descended a few steps, they saw a light, which gradually increased till they reached the lower chapel, which was lit by a multitude of tapers. This crypt had somewhat the aspect of a prison: it was bare, without either pictures or *ex-votos* such as abounded in the upper chapel. There was simply an altar or table of white marble, rudely but curiously carved, attached to the wall. On one corner of the altar, around which were a score or so of these nomad people, who are to be seen everywhere but live nowhere, Frederic pointed out to Renée a square box or case of very humble appearance, in which, through thick glass and the mist produced by the smoke, could be seen, indistinctly, some linen, mingled with shapeless objects which might have been bones.

"Those are the pretended relics of Saint Sarah," said Frederic. "But do not the heat and the oppressive odor inconvenience you?"

"No; let us go on," said Renée, bravely.

This was not an easy thing to do, for a compact group pressed round the case, where a young woman, whose ebony locks fell in disorder over her shoulders, was holding a half-naked infant, forcing it to press its lips fifty times, at least, to the glass covering of the supposed relics. Other children were dragging themselves about on the floor, scraping up with their nails the wax that had fallen from the tapers. They afterwards chewed it up, made it into hard balls, and brought it into one corner of the crypt, where the bony and withered hands of several hags were stretched out from the dusk to receive it.

Renée observed curiously two gypsies who, as motionless as bronze caryatides and with nothing animated about them but their eyes, knelt on either side of the altar, each holding an immensely thick candle, and then turned her attention to the children on the floor, and asked Germaine what they were doing.

"As you see," said Germaine, in a low voice, "they gather up the wax to bring it to the sorceress of their tribe—"

"The sorceress!" exclaimed Renée, with an involuntary shudder. "Is *she* here?"

"Look over in that corner."

Renée looked, and saw, crouched in the gloom, an old woman whose basilisk gaze was fixed upon her.

"Come away!" she said hastily; "let us go out. It is too warm; I find the air oppressive."

"You surely are not well, dear," said Germaine. "How pale you look!"

"I am stifling," she replied.

Germaine and Frederic almost carried her, rather than accompanied her, out of the crypt. The air was pure; the moon shone out in a cloudless sky. Renée looked around, put her hand to her forehead, and sighed deeply.

"Mademoiselle," said Frederic, "I trust this is only a passing faintness. Is it likely to continue?"

"No, no," she said, "I am quite well now."

"What was the matter, dear Renée?" asked Germaine.

"I am almost ashamed to say that I was afraid."

"Afraid of what?"

"Of that horrible sorceress, the same one we saw this morning. She hooked her talons, and looked askance at me."

"You need not have been afraid with me," said Frederic, half-unconsciously putting his hand to his sword.

He immediately uttered an indignant exclamation. The golden tassel of his sword-knot had disappeared; only a piece of the cord remained. It had evidently been cut by a snip of the scissors.

"It is too much!" cried he. "And these scoundrels shall find out that they cannot so insolently rob
an officer of the King."

Just then a gypsy appeared at the door to pass out.
Frederic cried:

"Go back again; no one shall pass here."

The man disappeared.

"What are you going to do?" asked Renée.

"Wait till my uncle comes up, and go down to
give these rascals a lesson."

"Alone?"

"No, with this for my companion," said he, touching his sword.

"Oh, I implore you!" cried Renée, clasping her
hands. "There are at least fifty of them below."

"Were there a hundred, I should not stop to
count."

"Be careful," said Germaine, "or you may get
into trouble."

But the young officer would hear nothing.

"Well! what's going on here?" said the Commander, in a half-jesting, half-vexed tone, as he
appeared. "I have been looking for you below,
and waited as long as there was any one in the
crypt; then, seeing that you must have left, I came
up."

"What, you say there is no one in the crypt?"

"No one at all." said the Commander. "One of
the gypsies who had gone out came back, and said a

few words to the bearers of the candles offered by the
new queen. Immediately the lights were put out,
and the Egyptians disappeared like a flock of birds,
leaving me alone in total darkness."

" How did they get out ? " inquired Renée. " No
one passed here."

" Fool that I am ! " exclaimed the young officer,
stamping his foot, " I forgot the staircase leading to
the church. Of course, these rascals escaped that
way. I am robbed ! "

" Console yourself, my dear nephew," said M. de
Forton; " I have lost a silk handkerchief."

" We cannot let such a thing pass," cried Frederic.
" What are you going to do, uncle ? "

" Buy another handkerchief, nephew," said the
Commander, in a tone so grave and so convincing
that the two young girls burst out laughing, and
Frederic restored his sword to the scabbard with a
sigh.

" This pious visit will cost me fifteen pounds eleven-
pence," said he.

" I am really distressed to have been the cause of
your loss," said Renée.

" The fault is ours," said M. de Forton. " We
should have known how much we can depend on the
honesty of these pilgrims. Every year these thievish
creatures come here in great numbers, bringing such
magnificent candles as you have seen, and for which
they pay very high; but they indemnify themselves

for their expenses in the lower chapel by their profits in the upper chapel. Whenever a new queen is proclaimed in the crypt of Saint Sarah, they reap a rich harvest of purses, handkerchiefs, watches, and all kinds of articles, from the most valuable to the most trifling.''

'' Yet,'' said Renée, '' I saw the children scraping up wax from the floor, which is no doubt used in making new tapers.''

'' Permit me, fair lady,'' said the Commander, '' to rectify an opinion which is quite natural for one who is not familiar with the customs of our country and of that accursed race. This wax picked up from the pavement, together with candle-ends stolen from the upper chapel, is melted with oil, amid certain superstitious rites, accompanied by incantations. It is then used in witchcraft and other diabolical practices.''

This conversation was interrupted by the sound of chanting which broke in upon the silence of the night. It was the pilgrims in the upper chapel, who had assembled around the relics, exposed during the night, to renew their supplications to their powerful intercessors, asking them to obtain the grace which they had come hither to ask. Through the open door they could perceive, above the close mass of heads, the light of the tapers and the upstretched arms of the kneeling multitude. Renée paused an instant, spell-bound by this consoling sight, which

effaced from her mind the painful impression produced by her visit to the crypt.

The voices sang:

> "Arriban de luen, pécaire!
> Pleu d'amour et de respet,
> O patrouno di pescaire!
> Pour nous traire a vosti ped!"*

Then there was deep silence, for prayer had followed upon the hymn, and only the noise of the
neighboring sea was heard, its waves joining in the
praises of God.

"Those good people will spend the night there,"
said Germaine to her friend; "to-morrow the sun
will find them still praying and singing alternately."

Renée was deeply touched. They all walked on
silently to the little house near the priory where they
had found lodgings. Just as they reached there the
voices were again heard in the distance, singing one
of the more familiar hymns:

> "But God's holy providence
> Into Provence
> Showed you the way."

Reneé was overcome with fatigue; but, instead of
going to bed, as soon as she had reached her little
room she threw herself on her knees and, bursting
into tears, cried out from the bottom of her heart:

---

* "We sinners come from far!
Full of love and respect,
O Patroness of fishers,
To thy feet we come!"

" May Thy providence, O my God, enable me to find in Provence, whither Thou hast brought me, the way which I seek ! "

This way was that of her vocation. Early deprived of her mother, Renée de Blésignan had been confided by her father to the religious of the Convent of St. Praxeda to be educated.

Of a nature at once gentle, poetic, and loving, the child felt a special attraction for prayer, and this tender piety increased as she grew older. " Our Renée is like a lily which is gradually unfolding," said the Superior, charmed with the good dispositions of her favorite pupil. It is generally supposed that piety means a sort of forced gravity and self-concentration. Nothing could be farther from the truth. Any one familiar with religious, especially those who follow the most austere rules, are aware that, on the contrary, prudent directors regard as a sign of a non-vocation that natural melancholy which the world attributes to those who are separated from it. Renée had in the highest degree the excellent quality of an even disposition. Simple, cheerful, and even merry, she adapted herself to all her companions and made herself universally beloved.

The Superior of St. Praxeda, a woman of cultivated intellect and of ardent piety, was well aware that the Marquis de Blésignan, who, of his three children, had only Renée remaining, would desire her to marry young, and settle in the castle of Nyons,

to be the solace of his declining years. Too prudent
and discreet to interfere with his plans unless God
should ordain otherwise, the abbess studied the disposition of her pupil, cultivating heart and mind
alike, while carefully abstaining from advising her to
any step which the providence of God did not mark
out in an unmistakable manner.

When Renée, at the age of sixteen, left the convent, she said to the nuns:

" I am not leaving you forever: I will return."

" My child," said the abbess, " obey God and your
conscience. You can save your soul anywhere, and
Providence does not require that all young girls
should consecrate themselves to a religious life."

" I feel that I will come back," said Renée.

" Sometimes we can do more good in the world
than in the cloister," said the nun, with the calm
dignity that nothing had power to ruffle. " May
your good angel watch over you. Adieu, my
child."

That very evening the Marquis set out with his
daughter for Nyons. Notwithstanding the pleasure
which he felt in the thought that his daughter—and
such a beautiful and charming daughter, who would
do the honors of the castle so admirably—was returning with him at last, he was thoughtful and almost
sad.

The abbess had spoken to him, for she had divined
what was passing in Renée's mind before the young

girl had told her of it, and felt bound to acquaint the Marquis with the result of her observations.

M. de Blésignan was a Christian and had a profound respect for religious, men and women, but he had never dreamt that his daughter would want to be a nun. His selfish paternal love revolted against the thought.

" *Cornebleu !* " cried he, " if I thought that Renée dreamt of such a thing, I would marry her to-morrow."

" That is the affair of your own conscience," said the abbess, with her grandest air. " My duty was to let you know; it is for you to act as you think best. Allow me to observe, Monsieur, for I have seen striking examples thereof, that it is dangerous for parents to oppose the will of God, and to seek to take from Him a soul which He has chosen. God is more powerful than we, Monsieur le Marquis, and what we obstinately refuse Him He often takes from us."

And rising, the abbess bowed profoundly and left the room.

Several weeks passed, and no subject of dispute came up between father and daughter. Renée was always gay, affectionate to her father, and unostentatiously pious. By her grace and distinction of manner she charmed all the people of rank who came to the château, and by her goodness made herself idolized by all the servants and tenants.

Did her father desire her to attend to the duties

of the household, she performed them with the precision of a long-tried housekeeper; did he wish her to
ride with him, she rode to perfection; did he bring
her into society, she shone there by her natural elegance and an unaffected gayety which caused her to
be much sought after and admired. Renée made
but one exception. She did not absolutely refuse
to go to the theatre, but she asked her father as a
favor not to take her there. He, so imperious, so
unbending, riding the hobby of his rights, did not
insist. She overcame his strength by her gentleness,
and inspired him with such unwonted timidity that,
whereas he had resolved to declare his sovereign will,
he dared not open his mouth on the famous subject
of vocation. Nor did Renée allude to it. She instinctively felt that he would be inflexible upon this
point; while he knew that she would yield to all his
desires except that one. Their life was apparently
peaceful; but it was only a truce. Sometimes the
young girl hinted this to him, as when he asked her:

" Would you not like to go to this ball ? "

" Yes, because I know you wish me to go."

Upon one occasion he sent to Lyons for a costume
more elegant even than usual. She wore it, without
making the slightest objection. At night, when all
the company had departed, he complimented her on
it, saying:

" You looked charming in that dress."

" I am glad you liked it," she said, " for pleasing

you is a compensation for the trouble of putting on
and wearing so complicated a dress."

She spoke thus in all sincerity. Her heart was not
in the world; she shone there, but she did not care
for it, and much preferred a solitary walk in the
mountains, with her father as guide, to all those inane
assemblies, where even vanity often suffers more than
it triumphs.

Still, self-controlled as she was, Renée had moments of despondency, which her father was not slow
to perceive. These foggy days, as she afterwards
called them, were rare indeed, though not so rare
but that they told upon her health, and the mountain
air, which should have brought color into her cheeks,
only made her paler and paler. M. de Blésignan was
distressed beyond measure. An old physician of
Nyons, and a friend of the family, who had come to
the château only in this latter quality for the past
fifteen years, as M. de Blésignan did not know the
meaning of the word sickness, replied, when the father
questioned him upon his daughter's paleness:

" Her constitution is good; Mademoiselle de Blésignan is not ill, but I mistake very much or she has
something on her mind."

" What could it be ? "

" Some inclination thwarted—how should I know? "

" You are sure she did not confide anything to
you ? "

" Nothing at all."

The conversation ended there, for the Marquis changed it so abruptly that the doctor said to himself: "The Marquis knows what the trouble is."

A few weeks after he was going up the mountain to visit a patient, and as he climbed the steep road, reading as he went, he heard his name called. He turned, and saw M. de Blésignan, with his gun on his shoulder, coming up behind him.

"Have you had good sport, Monsieur?" asked the doctor.

"A hare or two, but I was not thinking much about it. Tell me, doctor, do you suppose that an inclination thwarted could cause illness?"

"That depends upon the nature of the person."

"But putting things in the worst light?"

"Then it might cause death."

"*Cornebleu!*" cried the hunter, rapping on the ground with his gun. "And the remedy, doctor, the remedy?"

"Distraction, occupation, and especially travelling."

"Travelling?" said the Marquis. "We will try that."

And, throwing his gun over his shoulder again, he turned abruptly away, forgetting even to take leave of the good doctor.

A week afterwards the doctor went to the castle, to dine there, according to his wont, on the first Tuesday of every month. He was surprised to learn that the Marquis had gone, three days before, to Lyons with his daughter, and that the time of his return was uncertain.

But this journey had not the desired effect. Renée liked the tumult and bustle of large cities still less than the calm and quiet of the country. The only real pleasure she experienced at Lyons was going to pray before the shrine of Notre Dame de Fourvières. So her father brought her home. As he passed through Orange the idea occurred to him to go and visit his cousin, Madame de Lafare, who had recently been elected abbess of the Trinitarian nuns at Bolênes. Madame de Lafare, though an excellent religious, was still the *grande dame*. She greeted them cordially, and said, joking, to the father:

" Since the happy thought of bringing Renée here struck you, you had better leave her to us."

The "*Cornebleu !* " came to the Marquis's lips, but he restrained it.

" Would you not like to stay with us, my dear ?" said the abbess, addressing Renée.

" With my father's consent I would like nothing better, ma mère," said Renée.

" You hear, cousin. I demand your consent."

" We shall see about that later," said the Marquis.

" God does not like delays, cousin," said the abbess, still smiling.

The Marquis was enraged at his own rashness in falling into such a snare, but the harm was done. He

promised to bring Renée back, to have a talk with
the abbess, but meantime set out hastily for Nyons,
excusing himself to Madame de Lafare on the plea
of a message that he had received.

A journey to Marseilles, some months later, had
no better effect, though the Marquis scrupulously
avoided convents. His daughter, who had been so
delighted with the shrine of Notre Dame de Fourvières at Lyons, was equally charmed at Marseilles
with Notre Dame-de-la-Garde, patron of sailors. Of
all the balls at which she assisted none produced half
the impression made upon her by a chance meeting
with some thirty rude mariners, who, barefooted
and bareheaded, carrying lighted tapers, were climb-
ing the hill, singing litanies to the good Mother,
whose intercession had snatched them from the fury
of the waves, and before whose altar they were going
to hang, as an *ex-voto*, a miniature of their ship, the
St. Joseph of Martigues. After such a sight what
could she see in a review or civic procession, where the
municipal authorities paraded in red robes, preceded
by rod-bearers and lackeys? Even M. de Blésignan
himself had to admit so much. Yet the time was
approaching when the poor father would be obliged
to come to some decision. He knew it well, and
could not conceal from himself that his daughter had
made little progress in her affection for a worldly life.
Besides, Renée's health was far from improving.

" What are you doing to your daughter, Marquis ? "

said the prior of the Carmelites, an ex-officer of the
Guards, who had exchanged his uniform for the serge
robe of the Fathers of Our Lady of Mount Carmel.
" She is evidently homesick."

This remark, and many others to the same effect,
painfully impressed him, for he remembered the last
words spoken by the abbess of St. Praxeda, and his
own conscience seemed to whisper:

" God can take your child from you if you refuse
to give her willingly."

Still he persisted in driving away the thought. He
was not courageous enough to renounce all the happiness he had promised himself in the near future.

This state of things went on for some time longer,
when one day a messenger brought a letter to the
château of Nyons for the Marquis. The arrival of
such a document now is a matter of little moment, but
then a letter produced a sensation; it was only written
on rare occasions or to convey some extraordinary intelligence. However, the Marquis easily guessed
whence it came, and by whom it was written. The
word Provence, inscribed in great red letters, showed its
whereabouts, and the crest of the Commander, stamped
upon the seal, left no room for doubt as to who was
his correspondent. Yet it was not till he had turned
it over and over again, and weighed it in his hand,
that he decided to break the seal and read what his
old friend had written. After a preamble, which was
as ceremonious as all that he said and did, the Com-

mander announced to his old friend that on such a
day and at such an hour—almost at such a minute, so
precise was he in his details—he would arrive in
Avignon, where he would put up at the sign of the
Trois Rois Mages,* in the Rue Calade, so called because it was entirely paved; that unless urgent business
prevented M. de Blésignan from being there he would
be most happy to see him, and converse on matters
of the deepest importance, the successful issue of
which would much rejoice him, as it would bind still
closer the ties of friendship and of kinship which
had long united the two families, and by which he,
on his part, set infinite store. A whole page was devoted to protestations of this nature, written in a
stiff, close, large handwriting, where the letters were
all under arms, and in which the lines preserved their
exact parallels and their equal distances with the
regularity of a battalion of Frederic the Great's
grenadiers. The second page was the rear-guard of
this superb main wing, or what we might more simply
call a postscript, the object of which was to announce
the accidental return for a few months' leave of his
nephew Frederic, of whom he drew a most flattering
portrait. His nephew and future heir, he said, was
a young man of great promise; but that his mother,
who was a widow, and naturally anxious to keep her
son with her, would renounce his brilliant prospects if

* The Three Kings or Magi.

an alliance presented itself such as his fortune and
ancient name made desirable.

M. de Blésignan had never shone by his skill in
guessing the riddles with which the new patriotic
journal embellished its last page, but this time he
found the key to the enigma at once, and felt a lively
pleasure in the thought that a man of the tried valor
of his old friend the Commander was coming to his
aid. It was not altogether chance, therefore, that
caused him to meet M. de Forton in Avignon, nor
altogether the persistency of the latter which had
made him promise to bring his daughter to Camargue about the time of the pilgrimage.

This little comedy, played for the benefit of the
public, and every detail of which was carefully repeated at Nyons, as well as at Camargue, was really
the result of a conspiracy in which Madame herself
was prime mover. The noble lady had sufficient
tact not to represent herself as the soul of the movement, for she knew that the best means of interesting the Commander in its success was to leave him
under the impression that his diplomacy had alone
been able to conquer the young girl's passive resistance. Yet, in spite of the penetration of our châtelaine, who, in the first place, shared the illusion of all
mothers as to the merits of her son, and who, in the
second place, was of those who, because they desire
a thing ardently, feel certain of obtaining it, she allowed her hopes to be raised by the simple, affec-

tionate word which Renée had spoken to her in the
church. She totally mistook the import of such a
title bestowed upon her at such a moment.

M. de Blésignan was also charmed with the effect
of his trip. His daughter had not been for a long
time so unaffectedly gay as since her arrival in Camargue, where everything seemed to please and interest her—nature and the people, especially Frederic, whose witty and sprightly conversation amused
her infinitely.

The Marquis repeated a dozen times a day to the
Commander:

"*Cornebleu!* he is a splendid fellow; he has a
superb figure, a fine face, full of life and spirit, and
wears his uniform to perfection. He reminds me of
what I was at his age."

M. de Forton did not answer, but smilingly took
a pinch of tobacco, and dispensed with a prodigal
hand the treasures of his somewhat old-fashioned
courtesy to the fair lady.

The next day it would be too late to think of setting out after the blessing of the relics; and they did
not like to leave before, as Renée was most anxious
to see the end, and the touching ceremony of the
procession to the seashore. It was therefore decided
that they would wait for the removing of the relics.
This last episode was. perhaps, the most touching
and most dramatic of all.

After Vespers and Benediction in the evening the

pulley was let down again to the altar, where hitherto
the precious relics had been exposed; the Saints were
going up into their upper chapel for another year.
Some of the infirm were cured—they were, of course,
the few; the others saw with despair their last hope
vanishing. Cries and tears broke forth on all sides;
the more ardent threw themselves before the reli-
quaries and embraced them as if they would not let
them go; the pulley was tightened, the cords stretched,
but the groups of suppliants still clung to the sacred
coffers. Vain efforts! already they were losing
ground and must soon let go. But the letting go
was accompanied by sighs and tears; all hearts and
hands were outstretched towards the relics. Prayers,
hopes, and wishes rise with them; it is the last incense sent up to the vault above.

" Great servants of God, who have lived but for
Him, who have consecrated your lives to the praise of
His holy name," said Renée, in her heart, " forget
not that she who now implores you asks only the
grace to imitate you. And since you have brought
her here, grant that in Camargue, which you have
sanctified, she may obtain the favor which she asks."

Her whole soul was in these words. The Saints
heard them, and found them pleasing, for the sup-
pliant seemed to hear a voice, which said:

" Have confidence ! Your prayer will be heard.'

A great calm fell upon her spirit. When she came
out of the church, her face seemed as if transfigured.

" Well, my child, how did you like our pilgrimage ? " said Madame.

"Ah! mother, it is beautiful and consoling. I am
so glad that I came here with you," said Renée,
taking one of Madame's hands and kissing it affec-
tionately.

This time Madame could not have been mistaken.
Renée had certainly said " mother." The Commander silently clasped his friend's hand, and the
friend himself, under pretence of examining the carved
lions at the door, turned away. to hide the tears of
joy which rolled down his face.

" If you are not too tired," said Frederic, " we
might go to the city gates to see the departure of the
pilgrims."

" With all my heart, if Germaine is willing," said
Renée.

" Perfectly willing, dear,'· said Germaine. " Let
us go at once. "

The sight they saw repaid them for their trouble.
All around the walls were what seemed like bees
swarming around their hive. Tents were being taken
down, stakes pulled up, while the neighing of the
Camargue ponies, being mounted by the guardians,
was only equalled by the concert of asses and mules
being harnessed by their owners. Whilst the vehicles
were filled to overflowing, the pilgrims, the real pilgrims, who had come hither on foot, had already
formed into a long, black line, proceeding in the di-

rection of the Rhone, the course of which most of
them followed as far as Albaron. Singing they had
come, and singing they departed, and of their hymns,
gradually dying away in the distance, only the refrain, which was sung in chorus, reached the ear:

> " Belli santo
> Ravissanto,
> De tout cousta,
> Touti li pople encanto
> Venon per vous canta." *

" I need hardly translate you these lines," said
Germaine.

" No, I quite understand them," said Renée, herself translating them.

At that moment, with a great noise of trumpets
and bells and horns, the whole gypsy tribe moved off.
The new Queen of Egypt, seated beside the King in
the last cart, showed her white teeth in a profusion
of smiles, and sent kisses to the right and left. As
they passed the group in which Frederic stood he took
off his hat and bowed.

" What are you doing ? " said the Commander.

" Paying military honors to your *foulard* and my
sword-knot," said Frederic.

---

* " Beautiful, ravishing saints,
With all their soul
The people enchanted
Come to sing your praises."

CHAPTER VII.

MARITIME CAMARGUE.

THE Rhone!" cried Renée next morning when she suddenly saw the blue waters thrown like an azure scarf upon the yellow sand, which, like an undulating drapery, surrounds the little town of les Saintes; "I thought it was behind us."

"That is not the Rhone, dear," said Germaine, "but a fragment of one of its former arms, which now has no communication with the sea."

"True, this water has no current; one would think it was asleep," said Renée. "Yet the sea is not far off; that is it shining before us."

Germaine laughed.

"What you take for the sea," she said, "is the Imperial, after which comes the Malagray, another little stream, that is itself but a continuation of the Valcarès."

"Then we are not returning by the same road," said Renée, who, in this network of water and sand, sought her whereabouts in vain.

"You came to see Camargue, fair lady, and to gratify your desire, which is law to me, I have changed

our course in order to show it to you under its fairest
aspects," said the Commander, who, now full of hope,
exhausted himself in devising an uninterrupted series
of pleasures and amusements for the daughter of his
old friend.

"You are far too kind, Monsieur, and I am quite
embarrassed at the trouble which I give you," said
Renée.

"My reward is in your gratification," said M. de
Forton.   The gypsies had fortunately left him his
snuffbox, into which he now dipped, at the same time
making his horse go through the evolutions indicated
by the *parfait écuyer français*.

" *Cornebleu !* my dear Commander," said the Marquis, who was watching his friend's movements, "you
ride as well as you did at twenty years.   Really,
Madame," he added, turning to the châtelaine, "I
think your country is a fountain of perpetual youth
for men."

"It is to be regretted that it is not the same for
women," said Madame, smiling at the Marquis's
enthusiasm.

"Such a regret on your part, Madame," responded
the Marquis, promptly and with a profound bow, "can
only be explained by the anticipation of a distant
future."

" The compliment is delicately put, Monsieur," said
the lady, "but happily I have no illusions upon that
score.   If I had kept any, my mirror would have dis-

pelled them long ago; but that is little matter, and my
only anxiety now is, not my own future, but that of
our children "

"For that future, Madame, I have faith in Camargue, and still more in the attractions of those who
inhabit it."

"In fact, things are going pretty well," said M. de
Forton, bending over to his friend, and pointing to
Frederic, who was riding gayly along beside the two
girls.

They were now but a few paces from the river, upon
which a vessel was dancing lightly, waving its white
sails in the breeze. In the distance they could just
distinguish a canoe, urged by two vigorous oarsmen,
which soon disappeared behind the point of la Rédon-
nière.

At sight of the cavalcade two fishermen, standing
upon the shore, chatting with a group of guardians who
were seated on their white ponies, at once began to
haul in the vessel as close as possible to the shore.

"One would think they were awaiting us," said
Renée, pointing them out to her cousin.

"That is just what they are doing," said Germaine.

"They are our fishermen and guardians," said
Frederic. "I recognize Marius among them."

"And I am looking vainly for Thérésine," said
Germaine. "My uncle, who has thought of the su-
perfluous, may have overlooked the necessary."

"Is Thérésine what you call the necessary?"

"Not Thérésine exactly, but the provisions which she has in charge; and if, as it would seem, we are going to embark on that vessel, we shall run the risk of dying of hunger."

"And thirst," said Frederic, with a sigh. "The stream is broad, the trip delightful, but there are no inns upon the way."

"We shall catch some fish, and for our drink we shall gather the rain of heaven, as shipwrecked people do," said Renée.

"It is very romantic in a novel," said Frederic, "but in reality the stomach does not accommodate itself well to fiction."

"We shall have recourse to Providence, and God will be our aid.

"'Aux petits des oiseaux il donne la pâture.'"*

"To the birds, very likely," said Frederic; "but unhappily, as far as I know, we do not belong to that interesting family."

"'Et sa bonté s' étend à toute la nature,'"†

continued Renée, repeating, with the most melodious accent possible, those charming verses of Racine.

Still Frederic was not reassured, and hastened to ask Marius if there were provisions on board. The answer was not satisfactory.

---

* "To the young of birds He giveth food."
† "And His goodness extends to all nature."

"And the baskets in the carriage?" persisted Frederic.

"They are empty."

"Where is Thérésine?"

"She left this morning."

"Then," said Frederic, offering his hand to Renée, who was running about like a child on the fine sand, "my uncle has forced a fast-day upon us, and, frankly speaking, I think he would have done better not to infringe upon the rights of the Church."

Just then the carriage arrived, and M. de Blésignan and Madame got out.

"Take the horses back to the *Mas Rouge*," said the Commander to the guardians; "and you, Jean-de-Dieu, be at the salt-works of the tower of Valat with the carriage about five o'clock this afternoon: we shall all sleep at the Commandery to-night."

"It is now a quarter to nine," murmured Frederic; "we shall never reach the salt-works before three, at earliest. Why, it is longer than the Lenten fast."

"You fellows," said M. de Forton, addressing the fishermen, "must take us round by the islands between the Sansouire and the forest of Rièges, where we will get out and walk about a little."

Frederic's face lengthened so perceptibly that Germaine burst out laughing.

"It is sheer treachery," said the dragoon. "Had I suspected such a plot, I should have taken three months' provisions with me. We shall never get there before four o'clock."

"Fair lady, permit me to take your hand and assist you into the boat in which you are going to traverse our miniature ocean," said the Commander, leading Renée to the vessel, in which Madame de Marcoiran and the Marquis were already seated.

"Push off," said the Commander.

Marius obeyed with one blow of his boat-hook, adjusted the helm, while the two fishermen rowed with all their might and main to reach the place where the sails could catch the wind. They passed a whole bed of marine plants, a species of water-lilies with large round leaves, called by the fishermen water-pancakes, and of which the yellow flowers, supported by long green stalks, seemed to follow every undulation of the waves.

In the midst of this verdure, dotted by the spring with golden nails, darted in and out, like silver lightning sparkling in the furrow made by the boat, a multitude of little fish frightened by the noise of the oars, whilst above circled, with sharp, piercing cries, snow-white gulls, who, suddenly folding their wings, swooped down upon the fugitives, making a splash in the water, and reappearing suddenly like flakes of foam dancing on its surface.

The boat meanwhile pursued its course; it soon reached the point where it caught the breeze. To the green meadow succeeded the blue of deep water;

the boatmen raised their oars, and the sail, suddenly unrolling, veered round, sending the boat over so suddenly that Renée just escaped being thrown out by seizing the edge. But after that the motion, though swift, was so gentle that it seemed as if an invisible force were urging it over the surface of the waters, which, cleaved by the edge of the boat, divided, and festooned its dark sides with a light veil of gauze.

For the first time in her life Renée experienced being borne over the water by the gentle motion of a sail-boat. The novelty of the sensation, and the beauty of the picture which reached her eyes, enchanted her. Island succeeded to island, varying in form as in color, and in her delight Renée might have repeated to herself some such lines as these, written a century later:

> "Smyrne est une princesse,
> Avec son frais chapel,
> Et comme un riant groupe
> De fleurs dans une coupe,
> Dans ses murs se découpe
> Plus d'un frais archipel." *

It was truly a new world, at once charming and unexpected, this multitude of islands between the Valcarès and the sea; a perfect labyrinth of green and

---

* "Smyrna is a princess,
  With a chapel cool,
  And, like a laughing group
  Of flowers in a cup,
  From her walls are cut out
  More than one archipelago."

tenaer rush-beds alternating with its bluish rocks or
islands. the one empurpled by the saltwort waving
gently in the sunlight, the others gray, and starred by
those daisies of yellow gold which the salt-workers call
the *fleur d'amour.**

This world apart, full of poetry and sublimity, has
also its own particular population: white gulls, bluish
swallows, black water-fowl with coral legs running
lightly over the brilliant coating of salt deposited by
the sea, flamingoes with purple wings, gray herons,
ducks of all colors paddling about noisily, wild bulls
that, at the approach of the boat, raised their heads
and looked out from the rushes with an aspect at once
threatening and timid at the audacious travellers who
dared to disturb their solitude, and white horses neighing loudly and flying with mane flowing in the breeze,
raising a cloud of dust on their passage.

As they approached the forest of Rièges Renée's
astonishment increased. She was the first to perceive,
in a clearing, a tent formed by an awning stretched
over four trunks of trees, and beside it a bright fire,
around which were several figures, which were to be
seen passing and repassing through the colonnade of
pines. She pointed out the fire to Germaine and
Frederic, but neither of them knew anything about it;
the Commander took snuff and rubbed his hands, and
Madame smiled.   All at once the lynx eyes of
Frederic discovered Thérésine. He cried out:

---

* Love-flower.

"Why, there is Thérésine!" and his face brightened,
for Thérésine was the providence which supplied him
with his daily bread.

It was indeed Thérésine, who came to receive the
travellers, and offered Renée a superb bouquet of
coral-like flowers. The breakfast, served upon a
table-cloth spread upon the sand, consisted of viands
peculiar to the country: fish from the sea, and game,
rye-bread, corn-cakes, water as clear as crystal and as
cool as ice, in the *picous*, or earthenware bottles, hung
on the trees to keep them from the sun. The salt air
of the sea had sharpened their appetites. Boxes
served for seats, and Thérésine had forgotten neither
the wine furnished by the Commander's cellar nor the
coffee from the *Mas Rouge*. The weather was superb;
the heavens smiled upon the earth; a fresh breeze
stirred the pines, decorated with moss and long
streamers of seaweed, which hung in festoons from the
crooked branches whither the wind had carried them.

It required a few moments to appease their appetites, but soon the tongues were loosened, and toasts
succeeded to toasts. The Marquis drank to Madame
de Marcoiran, to his friend, to Camargue, to Germaine, to Frederic, to Thérésine, to his daughter, to
Marius, to the Sansouire, to himself. *Cornebleu!*
he would have drunk to the abbess of St. Praxeda herself could any memory of her have come to him in
such a moment.

M. de Forton drank a toast and composed almost a

madrigal in honor of the beautiful Iris, Mlle. de Blésignan, whom he proclaimed the sovereign of the
island of Camargue, and the brightest star in its blue
sky. This improvisation, meditated upon for two
days and carefully studied, was an immense success.
Germaine volunteered to crown the queen, and wove
for her a wreath all of flowers, with no thorns. Frederic drank to Renée through politeness, but to Thérésine through real enthusiasm.

In a word, the Commander's little surprise-party
was wonderfully successful, and the guardians of this
wild place gave three cheers, which were re-echoed
like thunder, when M. de Forton invited them, in the
name of Mlle. de Blésignan, to partake of the plentiful remnants of that plentiful meal, to the delicacy of
which their rude palates were little accustomed.

"Well, Monsieur le Chevalier," said Renée, as
they were getting into the boat, "will you believe me
now ? Was I not right in saying :

' 'To the little birds He giveth food'?"

"I admit," said the Chevalier, bowing profoundly,
"you are a great prophetess, my uncle a gallant Am-
phitryon, and Thérésine an illustrious cook."

Urged by the breeze the boat, directed by Marius,
beside whom sat his wife, glided lightly on in the
direction of the tower of Valat. The conversation,
at first noisy and animated, became quieter, toned
down by that gentle melancholy which is always in-

spired by wild and solitary nature, when the Commander, approaching Mlle. de Blésignan, asked if she would not sing something, no matter what, to gratify the joint wishes of all the company.

Her repertoire was not extensive, but she knew that in such a case it is better to do what one can without urging. Her voice was not powerful, but flexible and sympathetic. She sang one of the choruses from *Athalie* which she had learned at the convent, and which she sang with a peculiar charm. Every one applauded; but the Commander, who desired something more lively to raise their spirits, after having exhausted himself in praise of her effort, asked Germaine to sing.

"Sing the song of Magali," said Madame; "our dear Renée has already made such progress in Provençal that I am sure she will hear it with pleasure."

"I shall sing it willingly," said Germaine; "but the song is long, and as it is in two parts, Thérésine will sing the first, and I the second. Her voice is much better than mine, so you will lose nothing by this arrangement."

The Chevalier's foster-sister made many objections, feeling a certain hesitation as to taking any part in the amusements of her masters, but Madame insisted, and she began:

"O Magali, ma tant amado,
Mete la teste au fenestroun !
Escouto un pau aquesto aubado
De tambourin et de viouloun."

In a voice not quite so strong, but fully as harmonious, Germaine answered:

"Ei plen d'estello, aperamount !
L'auro es troubado," etc.

They continued thus to answer each other, verse by verse, while the boat sailed lightly on, and the chopping of the waves against the shore mingled with their strain of music. They had scarcely finished their song, which was interrupted by constant applause, when they arrived at the salt-works at the tower of Valat. They had come so rapidly that the horses were barely arrived. With them had come a guardian sent from the Commandery, bringing a letter for M. de Forton bearing the arms of the municipality of Arles. The Commander broke the seal, read it hastily, and said to the Marquis:

"My dear Blésignan, here is a letter to which I must at once reply. I ask your permission to stop here long enough to write a few lines in pencil, as pen and ink are unknown among the salt-workers. Meanwhile the horses will take breath, and my nephew, who knows the works, will do the honors and serve you as guide."

To any one who has never seen salt-works the immense tessellated plain, each square of which forms a cistern filled with water, clear or of a deep pink color according as it is more or less saturated, and separated from each other by little banks, or *queyrels*, opened

at stated intervals by sluices which carry off the fresh
or salt water alternately, is really a curious sight.   All
these right lines, running parallel with each other,
and cut square by other perpendicular banks, consti-
tute the workshop where evaporation takes place
every year, especially in August.

Frederic and Germaine had long been familiar with
the various operations necessary in the making of
salt.   They explained to their cousin the use of these
embankments, which serve not only to form squares
or compartments, but as paths for the overseers; the
utility of the sluices, which, as the water disappears
by evaporation, leaving behind its surplus of salt,
pour out a new stream of water, which in its turn
evaporates, till the precipitated salt is thick enough to
be removed.

"You see," said Germaine, "that the water is
almost red in some squares.   Those contain the sea-
water, which is not mixed with the other, and from
which the salt is taken somewhere about the month
of August.   The sun usually finishes the work of
evaporation.   Thick at first, this water grows crys-
tallized, and forms a thick layer of salt, glittering
like rose-colored ice, and so strong that not only can
it bear any weight, but to raise it an iron pick is
needed; then it is broken into masses something the
shape of paving-stones.   This operation is called a
levy, because at this time, when work is pressing, the
salt-makers, whose trade has hitherto required more

care than actual labor, collect in great numbers to remove the crystals, which they put in straw baskets, or *couffins*, containing about a hundred pounds of salt, rudely broken. These are heaped into pyramids, called *camelles*, such as you see yonder, covered with rush mats."

"I see only a line of little houses," said Renée, "and no pyramids at all."

"Those little houses, as you call them," said Frederic, "are precisely the *camelles*, or heaps of salt. See, at the far end are two, not yet covered."

"But are not those red pyramids made of brick?" asked Renée.

"No, they are of salt."

"But salt is white?"

"Yes, when the sun has bleached it."

"What gives it that red color?"

"A substance which is found in great abundance in sea-water—iodine; this evaporates very easily in the open air, giving forth a strong odor of violets."

"I thought I smelt them," said Renée, "and I was looking everywhere for those spring flowers, which we have in such abundance."

"Ah, those poor little flowers do not come here," said Germaine, "and we will do well not to stay too long ourselves."

"Why?"

"On account of the fever, my dear; we are in the very heart of its empire here, and it marks with its stigmata not only the salt-workers or men of the marsh who inhabit these regions, but even the revenue officers, who wander, night and day, around the salt-works to prevent smuggling.''

'' Poor people ! '' murmured Renée, whose compassionate heart felt pity for all misfortunes; '' they must lead a sad life here.''

'' You can judge by these specimens,'' said Frederic, calling Renée's attention to some five or six children, who at sight of the strangers came, barefooted and in coarse garments, in single file, along the *queyrel*, or narrow embankment.

'' Poor little ones ! '' said Renée, '' how thin and miserable they look. They are all skin and bone, and they have dark circles round their eyes. It makes one's heart ache.''

The little creatures now surrounded them, examining them timidly, not daring to speak, but offering them a little bouquet, or a shell, or a salt-crystal forming a rude representation of a heart, or a little rush basket filled with appetizing fruits which were quite unknown to Renée.

'' What is the name of that fruit, little one ? '' said Renée, pointing to the basket.

Instead of answering the child hid, frightened, behind her companions.

'' What is your name ? '' asked Renée, addressing the eldest boy.

'' Berzile,'' answered he, looking eagerly at a fifteen-

sous piece which the young lady had taken out of her
pocket.

" And your father's ? "

" Berzile."

" And your little sister, there ? "

" Manidette."

" What fruit is that in her basket ? "

He did not understand, and only stared at her.

" It is called sea-cabbage," said Germaine, " and
is excellent, these good people say, for fever, though
in reality it has never cured any one.   But your
French is out of place here; let me speak their own
idiom to them."

And, turning to the children, Germaine spoke to
them in the particular dialect of the Sansouire.   This
sufficed to untie their tongues: they began to chatter
all at once, and asked a farthing each, for the love of
God.   Renée enjoyed hearing them talk, and would
fain have gone over to examine the *camelles*, on the
other side of the salt-works.   But Frederic would not
hear of it, because, he said, the mist was there, and
the mist caused fever.

Germaine took the bouquet, Renée the fruit, and
Frederic the heart of salt; he paid royally for it,
giving half a crown, which, together with the coin
bestowed by the ladies, so delighted the children that
they did not even wait to say " Thank you," but
darted off, running and jumping, to bring this unexpected treasure to their parents.

The visitors now turned back towards the tower of Valat, which was their place of meeting, but as they passed a clump of rushes Renée suddenly gave a little cry of affright. The green cluster beside her was agitated by the wings of a large, snow-white bird, which emerged with great flapping and screaming.

" Do not be afraid; it is only a *gabian*," * said Frederic, quite unmoved.

" He is going to tell the good God of your charity," said Germaine; " see how straight he flies."

" One would think he was going to pierce that cloud," said Renée.

" In fact," said Germaine, " these *gabians* fly so high at night that the country people say they go up to heaven with news of all that has passed on earth during the day."

The horses being ready, the travellers hastened to wrap themselves up well in shawls and cloaks, and got into the carriage or mounted on horseback to pursue their homeward way.

It was long after nightfall when they reached the Commandery, a large house of gray brick surrounded by a palisaded courtyard. In this courtyard bivouacked guardians and soldiers, who had fastened their horses to the pickets, and, with their guns standing in sheaves around them, and the whole scene lit by the red glare of the *falions*, or rosin torches, lent to

---

* A bird peculiar to the place.

M. de Forton's square and massive habitation the appearance of a fortress besieged by the enemy.

A sergeant, in command of the men, approached to ask for the Commander's orders, whilst the other travellers entered a large arched room where, on an immense oaken table, lit by two copper lamps, was laid out a frugal supper. The table was drawn close to the fireplace, where a pile of fagots crackled and blazed. Though it was still quite warm, Madame advised her guests to approach the fireplace, and take a cup of black coffee as an antidote against the damp and the malaria.

Then she warned them, above all things, not to open their bedroom windows, for, said she, "you will be assailed by swarms of enormous mosquitoes, who will give you no rest; we are quite near the Rhone and the rice-fields, and, besides, are just at the season when this plague renders such precautions necessary."

The Commander came in just then, and they all sat down to table, more for form's sake than anything else, and did not remain there long.

"For," said the master of the house, "very early to-morrow morning we shall enter on a campaign. The trenches are dug, the enemy adroitly collected by our beaters in the Sansouire, and at sunrise we must engage in action before they have time to disperse. I hope, my dear Marquis," continued he, "that you will be of our party, for I do not venture to ask the ladies to take part in the affray."

" On the contrary, we are both going. Are we not, Renée ?" cried Germaine. " We already dream of laurels won, and only want to attack the enemy without delay."

" I shall be charmed to have you present, young ladies," said the Commander. " You will be as Venus and Pallas taking part in the war between the Greeks and Romans, and the Rhone will be witness of your exploits, as was the Scamander of those of the goddesses."

" In that case, brother," said Madame, rising, " I think it is better for mortals and divinities alike to retire and get a little rest."

" Thérésine will show you to your apartments, ladies," said the Commander, " and will wake you all when the moment of battle has come."

The chamber into which the young ladies were shown had only one bed, large enough for four, standing high up on twisted oaken legs, surrounded by a huge mosquito-netting, and a canopy at the four corners, whence fell long green curtains, which when closed together made a house within a house. The bed was such as was then found in all the châteaux, so high that one had to climb into it, on either side, by means of an upholstered chair, so large that it could comfortably accommodate two. Facing it, just between the windows, was a table covered with plans and papers; some book-shelves, laden with books, and extending to the wainscoted ceiling. Opposite this were some five or six cases, one of which specially attracted Renée's attention. As she went over to look at it Germaine took up the heavy silver candlestick from the table and brought it nearer.

"This is the room which my learned uncle calls his library, and those cases contain his collections; that one you are looking at is the various species of locusts which we are going to fight. You see, there are none wanting: *gigantea, ephippigia, grisea, verrucivora, viridissima, lineola, italica, stridula, grillus rotarius, grillus migratorius,* etc. They are gray, black, green, blue, yellow, or yellow striped with black; each regiment has its uniform and name."

"And such names, my dear! The barbarians who invaded Europe could not boast of any so frightful. But what is that, so finely written, on that piece of parchment in the corner of the case?"

"The first record of the military history of these terrible locusts," said Germaine, bringing the candle nearer; "they are some verses from the Bible."

And she read:

"'And the Lord said to Moses: Stretch forth thy hand upon the land of Egypt unto the locust, that it come upon it, and devour every herb, that is left after the hail. And Moses stretched forth his rod upon the land of Egypt: and the Lord brought a burning wind all that day and night: and when it

was morning, the burning wind raised the locusts.
And they came up over the whole land of Egypt.
. . . And they covered the whole face of the earth,
wasting all things. And the grass of the earth was
devoured, and what fruits soever were on the trees
which the hail had left, and there remained not anything that was green on the trees, or in the herbs of
the earth, in all Egypt.' " *

"With such petty instruments," said Renée,
thoughtfully, "does God accomplish the greatest
results."

And she knelt down at the foot of the bed to
say her night prayers. Next morning they were
sound asleep when Thérésine, opening the shutters,
let a flood of light into the library; the sun, just
ready to rush into space, was shedding its first rays
over the horizon. In the courtyard the horses were
pawing and neighing, and there was a great tumult
of voices—soldiers responding to the morning call,
guardians, already in the saddle, brandishing their
long tridents. Amongst them all was the Commander, everywhere at once, giving orders, sending
out scouts to gallop into the plain, assigning each
one his post, or listening to the reports of the or-
derlies.

The two young girls dressed quickly and went
down. Thérésine distributed black coffee to them

---

* Exodus x. 12-15.

all, the trumpet sounded the march, and the column of infantry and cavalry at once set out.

The Sansouire, towards which they directed their course, was fully a league in length to a half league in breadth; it was a vast plain of salt, absolutely bare, in the midst of which was what was called a *baisse*, a stream in winter and a rush-bed in summer.

The night previous the beaters had collected myriads of locusts, who were waiting in the long grass for the sun to dispel the mist and give strength to their half-formed wings.

But already a long line of women and children, armed with pine-branches, cut off their passage towards the threatened point, and an immense half-circle of guardians, soldiers, and farm-hands had ranged themselves round the Sansouire to force the enemy towards the left flank of the scene of combat, which was closed in by a deep *roubine* or stream.

It was towards this point that the leaders of the expedition at first proceeded. Laden with immense nets, called *seynes* or *traines*, came heavy carts driven by herdsmen and fishermen, escorted by a half score of fishermen of the Valcarès who preceded them. M. de Forton ordered them to unroll the nets along the stream, laying them flat upon the sand, and the guardians, armed with their spears, to alight and station themselves fifteen paces apart. Marius alone remained on horseback, directing the operation.

All these preparations, which Germaine and Frederic explained to her, interested Renée very much, while her father, to whom the idea of a battle had restored all his youthful ardor, brandished his riding-whip as if it were a sabre and, impatient of the delay, wanted at once to charge upon the enemy. Meanwhile the sun was rising in the heavens, and the mist growing perceptibly thinner.

"Forward!" cried the Commander, who, in the moment of action, like Turenne, became wonderfully cool.

And, setting off at a gallop, he stationed himself at the extreme end of the half-circle, facing the *roubine*. Then, rising in his stirrups, he cried out in a voice of thunder:

"Forward!"

Immediately each huntsman advanced, brandishing his long branch. But without waiting to hear more the Marquis, putting spurs to his horse, dashed across the Sansouire, waving his whip and shouting:

"Forward, *cornebleu!* Who loves me follows me!"

This charge had deplorable results. The horse dashed in among the rushes and so firmly imbedded its four feet that it stuck fast. The forward movement had to be stopped, and two guardians sent to extricate the too fiery Lord of Nyons.

He came back a pitiful sight from his adventure; his long riding-coat was covered with mud, slime, and locusts, some of which crept into his large

pockets, whence he drew them forth in seeking his,
handkerchief to wipe his face. Renée was somewhat
embarrassed, and the dragoon bit his lips; but M.
de Forton, with exquisite tact, seeing the general
embarrassment, advanced courteously towards his,
friend, and said aloud:

"Friends, the day will be propitious. Monsieur
le Marquis has taken some prisoners already. Let
us continue what he has so well begun. Forward!"

The mist had by this time completely disappeared,.
showing distinctly the shining wings of the locusts,,
gleaming like steel in the Sansouire. Their number,
not very great at first, increased as they approached
the rush-beds, where they covered the ground with
their heavy battalions. Some blows from the branches
had at first sufficed to disperse the more tardy ones,
but soon their numbers increased so that other means
had to be taken, such as drums, trumpets, the discharge of musketry, cries and shouts.

The frightened insects took refuge among the
reeds, but measures had been preconcerted to drive
them thence. Women and children, wading to their
waists in the mire, beat the bushes with such zeal
and so terrible a noise that the hostile army, seeing
an open space before it, made a sortie all together on
the *roubine* side. Pressed close there, bewildered
by the noise, enveloped in dust and smoke, and
seeing their retreat cut off by the fosse, into which
their vanguard had already thrown themselves, they

rose all at once, like one mass, with a sharp whistling sound of wings, which caused the horses to start, remained an instant suspended, like an opaque cloud, in the air, and, surrounded in the rear and on both flanks, made a forward movement to cross the stream. But at the same moment—for, an impulse given, these insects cannot immediately change their course —the fishermen and guardians, who had hitherto lain concealed on the other side of the stream, arose all at once, raising the poles upon which the nets were suspended, thus forming a diaphanous wall against which the flying squadron flung itself and became entangled, while the nets, falling suddenly, precipitated millions of them into the *roubine*, where they were drowned or crushed in an instant.

" *Cornebleu!* here is a victory in which I have had no part," said the Marquis, urging his horse over heaps of the slain. " I congratulate you, Commander."

" Thanks, my dear Marquis, though my victory is, unfortunately, such of which it may be said:

" ' To conquer without peril and to triumph without glory,'

for on our side there was no bloodshed.'

" Those are the best of all victories," said Renée, gently, " for they are *tearless victories*."

At this graceful allusion to a memorable fact in Grecian history the Commander replied by a bow full of respectful admiration, saying:

"And this victory is the more agreeable to me, fair lady, that it has caused you to display, by chance, another of those perfections which your modesty would fain conceal—I mean that of rare learning, combined with grace and beauty."

Though the first battle was so brilliant, the campaign extended over several weeks. The Commander therefore gave his orders for the next day, and the triumphant cavalcade returned to the Commandery, where breakfast awaited them, to which they did full justice after their early ride.

CHAPTER VIII.

THE "FERRADE."

THE days which followed one another at Camargue did not there, more than anywhere else, resemble one another. If Renée had had any doubts on this score, those which succeeded to that of the locust hunt would have dispelled the illusion. Germaine had, besides, predicted the sudden change which was soon to take place in the atmosphere, pointing out to her friend, just as they reached the *Mas Rouge*, on the evening of that memorable battle *without* tears, that the sun was going down in an ocean of fire. Not a leaf stirred upon the trees, not a wrinkle ruffled the surface of the stream, but the blue heaven was covered with jagged purple clouds, the flies harassed the wild horses, who ran madly about in the plain, the mosquitoes buzzed furiously, the swallows flew low with a plaintive cry, and all the animal creation seemed by their unwonted agitation to announce to each other the impending change.

"Unless I am much mistaken," said Germaine to ner friend, "to-morrow will be a day of forced rest for us."

"Why?"

"Because there is a *maestral** or northwester blowing up."

"Does it blow very hard here?"

"Hard enough to take the horns off a goat."

"Then the wind is as strong as at Avignon?" said Renée.

"Compared to ours the *maestral* at Avignon is a zephyr," said Frederic.

"When it blows there, it blows very hard," said Renée. "I have seen it carry off tiles and blow down chimneys."

"Here it blows houses down; in this beautiful Camargue of ours we never do things by halves."

"It would seem so. But tell me, does it last here, as at Avignon, for three, six, or nine days?"

"Exactly, unless it begins to blow during the night; in that case it lasts only till morning."

"I fear it will not begin at night this time," said Germaine, shaking her head. "But, after all, it is better for it to come now than at any other season; it purifies the air and rids us of those poisonous fever-laden vapors, which grow thicker every day. You do not have this wind at Nyons?"

"Not very much; you know it never goes up the valley of the Rhone farther than Provence; it is a real Provençal."

---

* *Maestral*, northwest wind blowing up from the Mediterranean.

" And like all Provençals," said Madame, with a
smile, " is hot-headed and good-hearted, a sort of
benevolent bugbear, a noisy reveller, who with all
his bluster does more good than harm."

" From your portrait of it, Madame," said Renée,
" I am quite disposed to like it."

Madame smiled, and thought:

" I am not surprised, for in the physical order it
resembles what her father is in the moral." And
she glanced at Germaine, who, guessing her thought,
smiled too.

For the rest, the *maestral*, which is such a bugbear
to strangers, has many friends in Provence. The
people call it the *grand mangeur de boue*,* because
it dries in an instant the rain-soaked earth. They
regard it as the best of doctors, knowing that it is
their only protection against the ravages of fever and
pestilence in the marshy lands where the slime,
heated by an ardent sun, loads the air with poisonous malaria.

In gratitude for the signal services it renders they
forgive its violence, though sometimes it is of long
duration. But its sphere is limited from Valence to
the sea; this being the only region in which it can
be useful, an ever-watchful Providence brings it in
existence and retains it there.

On this occasion, however, it was during the night

---

* The great mud-eater.

that this kind friend visited Camargue, but it came with full force. Instead of ringing discreetly at the door it announced its presence at the *Mas Rouge* by seizing upon a shutter which Renée had opened before retiring so as to be able to watch the sky, and using it as a knocker, with which it seemed determined to demolish the house. The first blow made Renée jump. She had just fallen into a peaceful sleep and was far from expecting this sudden attack; the second aroused the whole house. Annoyed at being the cause of this disturbance, and wishing to put an end to it, Renée rose, lit a taper, and attempted to close the shutter; but as soon as she opened the window the wind, blowing harder than ever, put out the light, sent handfuls of sand into her face, blew papers and curtains about, and rattled pictures and woodwork till Renée shrank back in affright.

Fortunately Thérésine, guessing in what direction the enemy had advanced to the assault, hastened to the breach, brought the shutter into subjection, lit her pewter lamp, restored order in the room, and reassured Renée, who, covered with confusion, had with some difficulty regained her bed. She was so terrified that the good Provençale tried to comfort her.

And, in truth, there was every cause for fear: the walls of the room cracked like the planks of a tempest-tossed ship; the trees, violently shaken, waved their great boughs fantastically in the light of the moon with a mournful sound; the wind, blowing terrible gales, roared, whistled, and shrieked without, growing calm a moment as if to take heart, and dashing with renewed fury against the house; the gravel was thrown in showers against the windows, and tiles were snatched from the roof and dashed to pieces.

"My God!" murmured Renée, "do you not fear that the house will be blown down?"

"Oh! there is no danger, Mademoiselle; the house has weathered many storms, and though the squall is brisker than usual this time, there is nothing to fear. The *maestral* knows us, and makes more noise than is necessary."

"Still it is very frightful."

"When one is not accustomed to it. But here we never sleep better than when it blows; it frees us from gnats, fever, pains, and, besides, we know that it is commanded to do all it does."

"You are right, Madame Thérésine; everything in nature obeys God; but, nevertheless, your country would be delightful were it not for this fearful wind."

"And that is just the reason why it blows here, and nowhere else, Mademoiselle—so my grandmother used to tell me."

"What used she tell you?"

"She said that when God created the world He had made Provence so beautiful, with its blue sky

and golden sun, its silvery Rhone and its azure sea
that, fearing lest the angels should desert heaven
to come and live in so fair a region, He took a half
score of mountains in his hands, and, reducing them
to dust, covered this lovely Provence with a thick
gray carpet. But, finding her still far more delightful than the rest of creation, He gave orders that the
wind should come betimes to raise the dust; and
the wind, which is a faithful creature of the good
God, blows with all its might to please Him. You
see there is nothing to be afraid of; so sleep well,
Mademoiselle. Would you like me to stay with
you ? "

" No, thanks, good Thérésine," said Renée, much
reassured; " I am not afraid now. I will take your
advice and try to sleep."

She slept long and profoundly, rocked by the tempest, which continued to rage; some one had to wake
her at breakfast-time.

All seemed well and cheerful, and greeted each
other with smiles; the conversation was lively, animated, sparkling; the Commander seemed ten years
younger and greeted Renée with a rolling fire of compliments, more spirited than ever.

" My uncle is very amiable this morning, is he
not ? " said Frederic.

" He always is," said Renée, " but to-day unusu-
ally so."

" Your presence has a good deal to do with it,"

said the officer, "but the *maestral* also counts for something."

"The *maestral?*"

"Why, of course; it gives us all a little flavor. My grandaunt, Madame de Saint-Veran, used to call it the mustard of the Provençal mind."

"How charming! but I did not expect the visit of so boisterous a friend and was a good deal frightened."

And she told her night's adventure.

"You heard it, dear," said Germaine, "but you neither saw nor felt it. Let us go up to one of the higher windows, from which you can see all the plain, and you will get some idea of what its face is like."

They went up to the second story to a large apartment that Thérésine called the drying-room, where all the windows were carefully stuffed, and whence the eye could behold on one side the river, on the other the broad stretch of country.

Renée stood still in astonishment.

"I can see nothing but smoke," said she.

And everything seemed in fact to have disappeared under a thick gray cloud through which only a dim light penetrated: harvests, fields, reed-banks, streams of water and sansouires, the very sky, were obscured by a dense cloud of sand raised by the wind and kept whirling constantly.

"Come here," said Germaine, leading her friend to a window opening on the river.

There the fog was less dense, and one could perceive the leaden waters rushing on in foamy waves,
and dashing against the bank over the bent and desolate reeds as if they would invade the whole island.

This storm had something weird and uncanny about
it. The wind made deep furrows in the dull, glassy
waters, or crested the waves with foam, which it
again dispersed in showers of spray; or it sent them
straying like waifs amongst the uprooted reeds. Above
this tumultuous disorder arose ever and anon the dull
roar of the waves dashing upon the shore, or a strange,
wild concert in which weird laughter, sobs or shrieks
seeming to be wrung from Nature in her agony, was
rendered more awful by intervals of strained silence.
Through it all were heard the plaintive bleating of
sheep, the long bellows of bulls, and the wild cry of
guardians busy collecting their flocks.

Renée remained motionless, contemplating in
amazement these convulsions of nature. This storm,
which raised the spirits of the Provençals, filled her
with mingled admiration and affright. It seemed
hard to believe that the *maestral* could have produced
such effects. When she went down again to the
drawing-room, she told Madame de Marcoiran of the
impression made upon her. Madame laughed.

" It will not last for more than three days," said the
Commander; "the wind is strong, but not solid."

"Not solid!" cried the Marquis. "*Cornebleu!*
I tried to walk down to the river, and I could not

even get through the garden; that brigand of a *maes-tral* threw sand in my eyes and shook me so that I could scarcely stand."

"No, my dear Marquis, not solid," repeated M. de Forton; "I know what I am talking about, and I can assure you that when the wind comes in squalls like that it will not last long."

"Meanwhile your crops will be destroyed."

"Some ears will be beaten down, but they will raise their heads again, and I prefer this tempest to calm weather."

"Your Valcarès does not seem so well pleased with it," said Renée.

"She is very ungrateful, then, fair lady," said M. de Forton, "because to-day's storm will give her an ample supply of locusts to feed her fish."

"Why to-day's any more than yesterday's?" asked the Marquis.

"Because this morning our beaters will urge them towards the river and force them to take wing. As the wind is stronger than their wings and blowing in that direction, it will drive them in by thousands."

"What! your people venture out in such weather as this?"

"Why, of course, my dear friend," said the Commander, "and I myself must go out presently to superintend their operations. If the *maestral* knows us, we must know it."

"I trust it will not blow quite so hard next Tuesday," said Frederic, "for, if I am not mistaken, the great *ferrade* of Mourefrech is fixed for that day."

"Oh, of course," said the Commander, "and I even forgot that Baron de Saint-Aignan had written me a very civil note asking us to be present, as well as our friends."

"We shall be delighted," said the Marquis. "I have often heard of the Spanish bull-fights and am most curious to be present at one. As it is not the sort of sport for women, I suppose the young ladies will stay at home."

"Oh, most assuredly," said Renée; "it frightens me even to think of so much bloodshed."

"On the contrary, my dear," said Germaine, "we shall all go, and I can assure you by experience that you will enjoy it very much."

"Do they kill the bulls?"

"They take good care not to kill them," said Madame, "for besides being too barbarous, it would be such a loss to the owners."

"Then these wild bulls belong to some one?"

"Certainly, my dear; we ourselves own some fifty or sixty. They are not tamed, but are left to graze at liberty under the eye of the guardians, and every herd or *manade* is one of the principal revenues of the land or marsh to which it belongs."

"If these bull-fights, or *ferrades*, are neither a hunt nor a fight, what are they?" asked the Marquis, who, less sensitive than his daughter, was disappointed at these replies.

The Commander was in a talking humor; he readily seized his opportunity, and in a somewhat lengthy conference, to which Renée listened with real interest, he discoursed learnedly on bulls and heifers, *bioulets*, or young oxen, and *védels*, or year-old calves. He explained the difference between a *ferrade* and a *muse- lade ;* the latter operation consists in weaning the calves by adjusting to their nostrils a wooden instrument so formed and so sharply pointed that the calf wounds the mother whenever she approaches, and is conse- quently received with such violent kicks that it is obliged to forego the milk, and be content henceforth with the grass of the salt meadows or the leaves of the rushes. The *ferrade* is a much more serious and difficult operation. After having separated the *bioulets*, or young bulls, from the herd, the object is to throw them down and mark them on the thigh with an iron bearing the initial or sign of the owner.

If this account so deeply interested the guests of the *Château Rouge*, the news brought by a messenger from the Baron de Saint-Aignan was received with the greatest enthusiasm in the kitchen of the farm. The news was that the proprietor of the herd, contrary to custom, had extended an invitation to all the guard- ians and herdsmen of the country, not only to assist as spectators at the approaching *ferrade*, but to dispute with his men the prize for skill and courage.

In Camargue, except salt-workers and revenue officers, the people were all bull-tamers or had been
such; hence the only emulation amongst them was
that of strength and skill.

This had given rise to a great deal of jealousy among
the guardians of each *terradon*, or estate—a jealousy
which often led them on to hatred. As in the old
heroic times, every estate had its Achilles and its
Hector, its Dares and Entelle,* iron-framed athletes
with broad shoulders, muscular arms, and backs of
steel, always ready to take offence, and to measure
their strength every time they met in village fairs, or
even within the limits of their own pasture-lands.

Hence, also, those extraordinary encounters where
blows fell like hail, where fists descended on the skulls
like sledge-hammers, where chests resounded like an-
vils, where an ardent multitude of spectators grew
enthusiastic over the heroes, furiously applauding when
the wrestlers closed against each other, knee against
knee, forehead against forehead, streaming with per-
spiration and covered with dust, each striving to throw
the other. The cries become almost deafening:
"Courage, Jean de l'Ourse!" "Take care, Meule-
de-Moulin!" "*Zou! Zou!* the herdsmen of the
Valcarès!" "Hold firm, Hercules of Faraman!"

The result of these desperate wrestling-matches was
told at evening in all the *mas*, and in all the cabins for

---

* Athletes mentioned in the Fifth Book of the Æneid.

four or five leagues round, and the young girls were usually the most enthusiastic, lavish in exaggerated praise or in bitter scoffs.

And whereas a guardian who was often victorious, whose name was in every mouth, might boldly ask the hand of one of these dark-complexioned admirers of strength, the vanquished, on the contrary, unless he wished to be ignominiously rejected, must needs go far to seek a wife.

Between the guardians of the cantons of Moure-frech (cold muzzle), belonging to the Baron de Saint-Aignan, and those of the pastures of Gouyères, the property of Madame de Marcoiran, there had long existed a rivalry which often found vent in scuffles between the herdsmen on sansouires of the *Grand-Mar*. Between these new Greeks and Trojans the subject of dispute was, not the beautiful eyes of Helen, but the valor of *védels*, *bioulets*, or *palusins* * with horns as hard as steel, who were committed to their charge. The Saint-Aignan and Marcoiran factions would attack each other on the slightest pretence, and if they observed a sort of armed neutrality, it was because their feudal lords, who were friends of long standing, declared that all aggressors, whosoever they might be, would be immediately driven from the domain.

" *Troun de l'air!* " cried Jean de l'Ourse, striking the oaken table with his ponderous fist, " we shall see

---

* *Palusin*, old bull

if Ourias of Mourefrech is *sans pareil* * for throwing a bull."

"Yes, we will let him see!" roared Couche-Dehors, a giant who had never slept on a bed, winter nor summer. "We will let the braggart see, and teach him, as well as José le Renverseur, that their bulls are only calves to ours; before the whole country, I will muzzle them as if they were lambs."

"Do not be too sure, comrade," said old Bernard, who was the wisest of the company; "they have this advantage over you, that they know their beasts."

"Nevertheless, at the races in Aigues-Mortes I took the cockade from their famous *Etoile du Soir*." †

"The same day that Ourias snatched the knot of blue ribbons from between the horns of your *Affronteur*," said Marius.

"Because he took me by surprise, and made use of treachery," said Couche-Dehors.

"He would not have dared look at the tail of the Terrible," cried Main-de-Fer.

"They never saw a real *palusin* except at a distance," said a chorus of voices.

The conversation was growing too animated. Thérésine raised her hand. The guardians respected her authority, and were silent.

"Let us have no more such shouting," said she; "you know Madame hates noise, so be quiet. It is

---

* *Sans pareil*, without an equal.   † Evening Star.

not by sitting at a table and shouting that bulls are
overthrown. If you are really stronger and more skilful than the others, you will show it on the *terradon*,
spear in hand. There will be three prizes of twenty
pounds each, and something better to drink than cold
water. Think well of it. You have until Tuesday to
strengthen your arms.''

These wise words calmed the storm which had been
ready to burst forth; but their vanity was piqued,
and during the following days they talked of nothing
but a complete victory over the enemy, who, on their
part, were determined to annihilate their adversaries
once and forever.

Throughout Carmargue the general topic of conversation was the approaching contest; it was discussed at
les Saintes, at Arles, at Saint-Gilles, and at Beaucaire,
and the lovers of sport rubbed their hands in glee.

The Commander, who was an intimate friend of
M. de Saint-Aignan, made a journey from the *Mas
Rouge* to the *Mas Brun*, two days in succession, in
spite of the inclemency of the weather, to arrange
with the Baron the programme of the forthcoming
festival, for which the three most celebrated tambourines from Arles, Saint-Rémi, and Rognonas-sur-
Durance were engaged. It was to be rather a tourna-
ment than a *ferrade*. Germaine could not sleep for
thinking of it, and Renée, who was at first so little
inclined for such a spectacle, began to share her
friend's impatience.

" She begins to like even the bulls," said M. de
Forton to his sister. " You will see; we shall make
her a real Provençale."

Madame smiled.

" I think they will be happy," she said.

There was not much difficulty in exciting the Marquis. He naturally required rather the rein than the
spur, and his friend had to use every possible argu-
ment to dissuade him from going down into the arena
and disputing the prize with the guardians.

The only anxiety was, whether or not the wind
would abate. On Sunday evening it fell. The two
following days were devoted to preparations.

On Monday all the guardians of Mourefrech,
mounted, spear in hand, and accompanied by their
doundaires, scoured the plain, driving all the beasts
indiscriminately, from the youngest calves to the oldest
heifers, into an immense park, where they were to be
kept till the appointed day.

This operation took a whole day, for with these
restless and suspicious animals it is not easily done.

Towards evening the first groups of spectators
arrived in carts, vehicles of all kinds, and on horseback, and, procuring what accommodations they could
for themselves in tents, under the more precarious
shelter of a tree, or in a pine-grove, in the shade of
which a species of tribune had been erected for the
Baron and his guests, they disposed themselves to
await sunrise.

The day rose bright enough; the sky, dotted with
tiny pink clouds, seemed like one of those curtains
of rose silk with which the Romans covered the
circuses, to arrest the rays of a fiery sun; the light
sea-breeze refreshed the plants exhausted by the rude
blasts of the *maestral;* all nature was in festal array.
Afar from the plain came carriages laden with spectators or horsemen, all wending their way to Mourefrech.

The party from the *Mas Rouge* comprised the
guardians, who, with the ends of their colored handkerchiefs, which they wore bound round their foreheads
under their felt hats, floating in the breeze, galloped
away joyously on their white mares, waving their
long forked spears, gilded by the rays of the
sun.

At a few paces behind these picturesque outriders,
came the battalion of honor, consisting of the Marquis
de Blésignan in grand array, blue coat with yellow
buttons, silk collar and revers, white waistcoat and
cravat, doeskin breeches, a three-cornered laced hat,
and soft leather shoes with silver spurs; the Commander, all in black, except his lace cravat; his
nephew, in full uniform heavy with embroideries;
and the two young girls, dressed alike in the Provençal
fashion: a skirt of sky-blue silk, embroidered in
silver, and corsage of black velvet with wide lace
sleeves, matching their neckerchiefs, and their hair
brought in bands over the forehead, and caught in the

back in a chignon, confined by a broad blue ribbon fastened at the side by gold pins.

In this Provençal costume, worn to please her friend, and manufactured by Thérésine's fairy fingers, Renée was truly lovely.   M. de Forton, on seeing her, cried out :

"Oh, Mademoiselle, I pity the mirror which, after having presided at your toilet, should be doomed to reflect your image no more till you return from the festivity where you will be queen."

"*Cornebleu !*" said the Marquis, proud of his daughter's beauty, "I begin to think that your true vocation is to become a Camarguaise."

These imprudent words brought a cloud to Renée's face, and she cast a gentle look of reproach at her father.

Germaine, on whom not the slightest shade of manner was lost, skilfully changed the subject, and sought by her gayety to do away with the effects of that unfortunate remark.

Happily, circumstances favored her efforts, and Renée's attention was diverted by the strange spectacle presented by the salt meadows, over which numbers of young men, arrayed in their best, rode their white horses with wonderful ease, sometimes having wife or sister, dressed in resplendent costume, behind them on the crupper.   They all hurried on, urged by the one absorbing thought.

As they approached the place set apart for the

ferrade, which was indicated by a long line of carts closely packed one against the other and for the most part covered with canvas, the bustle increased, the groups of people became larger and more noisy, whilst at the foot of almost every tree little fires were lighted, to prepare the coffee without which there can be no festivity in Provence.

As soon as the appearance of the guardians announced the arrival of the Marcoiran family, a little group of people came forward from the pine-grove to meet them. The group consisted of the Baron de Saint-Aignan, a man of distinguished appearance, his wife, and their children, a young girl of fifteen or sixteen, and two boys, aged respectively twelve and thirteen. After introductions and mutual greetings they all returned to the pine-grove, Mlle. Aloyse de Saint-Aignan riding beside Renée and wearing a costume so exactly similar to those of her two new companions that it was evident Thérésine had betrayed them. They soon reached the pine-grove. Renée expected to see the bulls already there, and was astonished, on entering a space closed in on either side by carts laden with spectators, to find it entirely empty except about the centre, in front of the tribune, where there were a lighted furnace and marking - irons with wooden handles. This space opened at either end into a bare and desert plain.

"I thought the bulls would be collected here," said Renée, looking all round.

"They are collected since yesterday evening," answered Mlle. Aloyse, "but the gates of the park in
which they are confined are kept shut."

"Is the park near here?"

"You can see it, about a quarter of a league from
here," said Mlle. Saint-Aignan, "there, where my
whip is pointing."

"That large black spot?"

"That spot is the bulls; nearer you can distinguish
the palisade which prevents them escaping; and those
horsemen galloping round are the guardians."

"At what time does the *ferrade* begin?" asked
Germaine.

"As soon as we have breakfasted, Mademoiselle,"
said the Baron, reining in his horse at the entrance to
a large tent under which was spread a table profusely
decorated with green.

They all dismounted, the servants taking the horses;
and, after new greetings, for in that rustic hall were
already collected about thirty of the most aristocratic
people of the vicinity, all seated themselves round the
sumptuously-appointed table.

The three young ladies were much surprised when
they were led to the seats of honor opposite their
hosts. Their places were marked by three large bou-
quets, tied with red and blue ribbons, the colors of the
two families; and they were still more astonished, even
Mlle. Aloyse, from whom the secret had been carefully kept, when they heard themselves proclaimed by

the Baron judges of the *ferrade* and the distributors
of the prizes to the winners.

"For our little entertainment to-day," said the
Baron graciously, "by an exception made in honor of
Mlle. de Blésignan's presence in our savage island, is
a sort of tourney, wherein the guardians of the *Mas
Rouge* and the *Mas Brun* will dispute the palm for
strength, courage, and agility before all these spectators."

This was said graciously and was warmly applauded.
After a repast, which was as pleasant as it was abundant, the guests repaired to the tribune, where three
sofas had been provided for the young ladies. The
multitude cried "Bravo!" as Mlle. de Blésignan took
her place, not without a certain emotion, between her
two companions and waited till it was time to give the
signal.

"Will you wave this little flag?" said the Baron,
giving her one of striped blue and red silk.

The young girl did as requested. Immediately the
drums and fifes struck up, the space was cleared as if
by magic, and none remained but a half score of guardians, the wearers of blue just below the tribune, the
red facing them. They wore jackets of soft leather
with short sleeves, leaving their brawny arms bare and
showing their powerful muscle; their waists were
tightly fastened by red or blue scarfs; their legs were
bare, their feet sandalled.

Every one was familiar with the names of these

men. On the red side there were Ourias, called
"Sans Pareil"; José le Renverseur, the "Serpent of
the Sansouire"; the "Rocher du Rhone" and the
"Viper of the Tamarisks." On the blue side were
Jean de l'Ourse, "Couche-Dehors," "Main-de-Fer,"
"the Arab," and "Trompe-la-Mort," all kings of the
land, all heroes of these saline steppes, who, according
to the number which they drew, were, in turn, to
attack and overthrow the enemy.

The gate of the enclosure was opened, and the
herdsmen sent forth one of the prisoners chosen in
advance. He was a young animal, a *bioulet*, as black
as jet, with sharp horns and thin legs. He gave a cry
of delight, and set off at full speed, with head down-
ward, believing that he was on his way to his solitary
pasture. But he had left the guardians out of the
reckoning. Quick as lightning two of them darted off
in pursuit and, circling round him, seized with infallible precision one of his horns in their iron spears, and
forced him into the arena. When he had reached
there the animal hesitated, fearing a snare, but, pricked
by the spears, finally rushed forward.

Who would dare to stop him? He was passing the
tribune at full gallop, when the Viper, with a shrill
whistle, sprang forward like a leopard, crying:

"The irons!"

Renée had not time to distinguish anything; she
only saw the bull lying on the sand, held motionless
by the guardian, who had him by the horn. The

marker advanced, and pressed upon the flank of the
vanquished the red fiery mark which burned the seal of
servitude into his white coat. Then the Viper unloosed
him, saluted and retired, whilst the bull, humiliated,
rose slowly, and went, without even daring to look
around him, to hide his shame in the depth of solitude.
The crowd applauded, and the victor, casting a defiant
glance at the blues, sat down and folded his arms.
Just then a second bull appeared. Jean de l'Ourse
did not spring forward, but advanced leisurely, his left
hand on his hip; and, regarding the animal with a
smile of contempt, he leaned his right hand heavily on
one of the bull's horns, at the same time tripping him
up. It needed no more.

" Mark him!" he said quietly.

Then, the iron having been applied, the guardian
released his prisoner and retired, shrugging his shoulders.

The reds were furious at this contemptuous treat-
ment of one of their *bioulets* by the terrible Jean de
l'Ourse, who braved them thus on their own *terradon*,
and at the plaudits of the multitude, who were good
judges of such matters.

" They have not won yet," growled Ourias to
Rocher du Rhone. " After the *bioulets* we will, if
needs be, bring out the *palusins;* there are five or six
not yet marked. It will bě risking our lives, but they
will have to risk theirs, and at the worst—"

" It is your turn, José, here is the bull."

The Renverseur did not need this intimation. He was already upon his guard. The animal was brilliantly overthrown, marked, and, like his comrades, he fled into the desert, bearing the insignia of servitude upon him.

Deeply moved, and terrified at first, Renée, seeing the apparent facility with which these giants on either side overthrew the bulls, had at last persuaded herself that it was the simplest thing in the world. The whole process apparently consisted in keeping to one side, to avoid the shock of the animal's approach, seizing him by both horns, striking the bull's left leg with the knee, pressing upon his left horn, and pulling violently on the right so that he lost his equilibrium, and the thing was done.

By the time the sixth bull arrived Renée began to find the performance, so often repeated, very monotonous, and the odor from the hides anything but agreeable. She was much more interested in admiring the dress of the mounted guardians, who circled about with their lances, to bring back the prisoners, and she heartily applauded the truly marvellous agility displayed by Marius, Thérésine's husband. Disdaining to enter the arena, where he would be matched against his inferiors, he circled in and out among the bulls on his snow-white mare, catching their horns upon the point of his spear with indescribable ease. Every one remarked him, so strong was the contrast between his grace and the brutal strength of the guardians, who were skilful and excellent horsemen, but far from equalling him.

The Baron de Saint-Aignan, amongst others, observed and applauded him, complimenting the Commander on his appearance, for it was pretty generally known that he was the Commander's adopted son.

"*Cornebleu!*" said the Marquis, "knights in tented field never wielded the lance better in their tourneys. It is a pity that fine lad is not a corporal of a cavalry regiment; he would be an excellent instructor."

Ourias heard all that was said, and foamed with rage. "*Troun de l'air*," muttered he, between his teeth, "wait till the *palusins* come, and we shall see."

At last the *palusins* came. The gate of the enclosure was thrown open, to give passage to a full-grown bull, with long horns and fierce aspect, who immediately rushed at Marius. The intrepid overseer recognized in him a foeman worthy of his steel; instead of flying or avoiding him, he steadied himself in his stirrups, put lance in rest, and waited.

With an animal of this size, when he attacked, there was no hope of turning aside and seizing him by the horn. The points of the spear were buried in the hide of the savage beast, who drew back with a roar, shook his head furiously, as if to free himself from the pricking, which had already marked his hide with two thin streams of blood. The shock was so terrible that the mare was almost overthrown, and the lance was

shivered like a piece of glass. As if he understood
that his enemy was disarmed, the monster rushed
upon him. But Marius was prepared. In the *palusin*
that Jean de l'Ourse was to overthrow, and he to
bring back to the enclosure, he had recognized the
Etoile du Soir, the strongest and fiercest beast in the
herd.

Ourias had kept his word, and revenged himself by
an act of treachery. It was he who had given the
signal to which the guardians of Mourefrech had gladly
responded, for the blues must be, at all hazards,
ignominiously defeated.

The spectators had soon discovered what they supposed to be an accident, occurring by mistake; they
all stood up, upon the carts, to have a better view.
As it was impossible to struggle against his adversary,
Marius was flying before him, making his horse perform a series of evolutions to avoid the attacks of the
Etoile du Soir, who, with head streaming blood, hair
bristling, and tail erect, made the sand fly under his
hoofs of iron.

However, Truphême, seeing the danger which
Marius was in, urged his steed forward, and flew to
his assistance.

"Your lance," cried Marius, "and be near to hand
me others."

Truphême obeyed, and gave it to him. Then
Marius, who had lost both his handkerchief and hat,
and whose black hair was waving in the wind, stopped

his horse again, and struck the bull in the forehead.

Dazzled by the steel, and stunned by the blow, the animal fell upon his knees, but at once arose. The terrible spear whistled again through the air, and the black giant, giving up the encounter, tried to fly in his turn. But his efforts were vain; Marius, almost standing in his stirrups, his face pale, his eyes flashing fire, like the veteran bull-tamer he was, showered repeated and terrible blows upon him.

The enthusiasm reached its height when the prisoner, forced to obey, appeared at the entrance of the arena. The Baron, fearing some accident, had already given orders that the way be cleared for the furious beast. All obeyed except Jean de l'Ourse, whose turn it was.

"Go away!   Go away!" cried hundreds of voices.

"I forbid you to mark this beast!" cried the Baron.

"Come back! Come back!" cried Frederic, Germaine, and the Commander.

But he never stirred. Crouching down like a tiger about to spring, his eyes bloodshot, he watched for his enemy, who, scenting him, pawed the sand and, lashing his tail, concentrated all his fury on this new adversary, showing his white star, already marked by a spear-stroke, between his smooth, bent, dagger-like horns.

"Escape! escape!   You will be killed!" cried the multitude.

All at once an angry roar was heard, and the black mass rushed forward.

" He will be killed ! he will be killed ! " cried Renée, closing her eyes. At last she ventured to open them.

Amid a cloud of dust she could perceive the bull, with the man hanging on to his horns; together they formed an indistinct mass, which rose and fell, fell and rose alternately. The roars of the furious beast were mingled with the hoarse breathing of the man. To separate them, to lend any succor, were equally impossible. In attempting to attack the beast it would be hard to avoid killing the man.

Suddenly a cry, thrilling as a clarion note, broke from the spot which was ploughed by the feet of the adversaries. The black bulk was seen to fall, and Jean de l'Ourse was descried lying prone on the head of the overthrown bull, which he now held down by the sheer weight of his body, and roaring:

" The irons ! the irons ! "

No one dared to approach, till Marius, leaping from his horse, rushed to the furnace, seized a red-hot iron, and marked the beast on the forehead, just above his white star.

Then there was a tempest of applause, and shouts of enthusiastic admiration; a shower of hats came into the arena, ladies waved their handkerchiefs. The excitement bordered on frenzy, and was redoubled when Jean de l'Ourse, his clothes in tatters, his face covered with blood, and his rough hair in disorder, advanced, supported by Marius and Truphême, to receive the well-won prize.

Victory declared entirely for the blues, they retired triumphant, whilst Ourias, spurring his horse, rushed off alone into the fields, furious and vowing vengeance.

" Well, my child, did you enjoy it ?" asked Madame of Renée when they got home that evening.

" Oh, Madame," said she, in a voice of deep emotion, " I am not born for such pleasures, and I still tremble at all that I saw."

CHAPTER IX.

"MAN PROPOSES, GOD DISPOSES."

NEVER had time seemed to fly for Renée as it did during these three weeks at the *Château Rouge;* the days seemed literally to have wings.

When they were not taken up by pleasure-parties, or little excursions prepared by the Commander, they were spent quite as pleasantly at the house, or in a little boat which Germaine was teaching her friend to manage. The whole family improved on acquaintance. Madame de Marcoiran, who was kindness itself, combined with a rare elegance of manner a charming graciousness, which made her beloved by all who approached her. Frederic, too, was good-tempered, sprightly, and lovable as well as clever, uniting the brilliant qualities of the head to the more solid ones of the heart. On first acquaintance the Commander might seem slightly absurd, and his politeness exaggerated; but, knowing him better, and finding him a man of the highest culture and a really interesting talker, it was easy to forgive his little peculiarities. Germaine was, of course, Renée's bosom-friend, and in her eyes perfection.

The Marquis congratulated himself heartily on the success of his friend's policy.

"*Cornebleu!* my dear Forton," said he, "it is to you I owe the happiness of driving those convent ideas out of my daughter's head, and of saving her life, I really believe, she has gained so much in strength and freshness since she came here; but yet you know, I go straight to the point, and this affair, so well begun, must be ended, and the sooner the better, as our stay has been already unreasonably long and beyond the bounds of delicacy."

"You are in too great a hurry, my dear Blésignan."

"No, no; strike while the iron's hot."

"Do you think it is very hot, Marquis?"

"Certainly! Your nephew is a splendid fellow, and suits me in every respect; with a fine name and moderate fortune, which is always an advantage in a father's eyes, he combines the manners and appearance of a finished gentleman, which is always a great deal in a daughter's eyes. Now that they know each other I really do not see that there can be the slightest objection."

"I hope so myself," said the Commander, "but I would rather be sure."

"There is a way, *cornebleu!*"

"What is that?"

"Let your nephew come and ask my daughter's hand."

"Permit me a remark, my dear Marquis. Besides

that it would be a manifest impropriety on the Chevalier's part to ask the hand of a lady who is on a visit with his mother, you must remember what unpleasantness would result thence in our friendly relations to each other if Mlle. de Blésignan should think proper to refuse him."

"You are right; you think of everything, and your objection is well founded. But what is to be done, then?"

"Your charming daughter must be sounded as delicately as possible, asked what she would think of such an alliance, have its advantages represented to her, and the question put confidentially how she would receive such a proposal if it should chance to be made—a thing which would not be very surprising, after a stay long enough for the Chevalier to—"

The Commander stopped. M. de Blésignan bit the end of his whip, which was always a sign of agitation with him; at last he burst out:

"All that is very fine," said he; "only, who is to undertake this confidential mission?"

"To tell the truth, my dear friend, I think it devolves upon you."

"Upon me? But I have not a grain of diplomacy about me."

"You wrong yourself, I am sure; besides, you are her father, and your authority—"

"She does just what she likes with me."

" Yet you are a man of strong will and uncommon
energy of character."

" With others, very true; but with my daughter
quite the reverse.   Oh, if she were a boy, *cornebleu !*
I would make her walk straight; and if she attempted
to kick I would teach her obedience and respect
with this," said the Marquis, shaking his cane signifi-
cantly.

" I do not doubt it in the least, my good friend,"
said M. de Forton, " but she is not a boy."

" Of course not ! of course not ! But have you
spoken to the Chevalier yet about our plans ?"

" No; I took good care not to say a word to
him."

" Well, when I have spoken, if he should not care
to—"

" A thousand pardons if I interrupt you, my dear
friend," said the Commander, " but there will be no
obstacle on Frederic's part, I can assure you.   I can
answer for him, and you may be certain that whatever wife his mother and I do him the honor to select
for him, even though she be not, like Mlle. de Blésignan, the most accomplished person in the world,
he will accept unhesitatingly."

The Marquis sighed.

" Ah," murmured he, " that is what they should
have taught her at the convent, instead of putting
it into her head that it was for her to decide upon
her own vocation, and telling me that if I refused her

to the cloister God would take her from me in one way or another.''

The Commander was not a very profound theologian, and openly declared the superior's words to be most imprudent; then, cutting all further digression short, he proved to his friend by unanswerable arguments that he must absolutely make up his mind to question his daughter before her good impressions of the place had been dispelled by her return to Nyons. The Marquis was really of the same opinion; besides, he believed his daughter favorably disposed, and much preferred to deal with this thorny question under such auspicious circumstances; only that he was not quite as completely convinced of all this as he chose to appear, and so tried to create difficulties for himself.   Forced from his last intrenchments by the Commander, he still thought of a means of escape.

" *Cornebleu!* " said he, fairly driven to the wall, "I will speak to her, of course; but she is never alone with me here, and to talk of such serious things—"

" You are right; I understand perfectly that you want to be able to discuss the matter calmly and without fear of interruption, a difficult thing enough when—"

" Say impossible, Commander, impossible !" cried the Marquis, clutching at this last straw.

" Will you speak to her to-morrow ?"

" To-morrow will be no different from to-day."

" The weather is fine; you can use the pretext of a visit to the *Mas Brun*."

" But the Chevalier and Mlle. Germaine will go with us."

" I will arrange a hunting excursion for my nephew with Marius, under pretence that we are out of game, and that Mlle. de Blésignan would like to have some bustard, which she has never tasted."

" And Mlle. Germaine ? "

" Her mother will need her at the last moment."

" But," said the Marquis, making a last desperate effort to escape, " neither Renée nor I know the way to the *Mas Brun*."

" I will send a shepherd to show you the way.   He will not understand French, and will, besides, keep a hundred paces behind or in front.   Shall it be to-morrow morning ? "

" Renée has done so much this week I fear it will fatigue her."

" The day after to-morrow, then ? "

" Very well; the day after to-morrow."

" So it is agreed."

There was no gainsaying it, the Marquis still hoped for some *contretemps;* but with the Commander he reckoned without his host.

" Mademoiselle, I hope by to-morrow evening to bring you home a bustard; since you have never tasted it, I want to make you acquainted with this

really excellent game," said Frederic, in the most
natural way possible, little suspecting the part he was
playing.

"Then you are going out shooting?" asked
Renée.

"My uncle has kindly given me permission to shoot
in the rice-fields belonging to the Commandery with
Marius, who is a splendid shot, and upon whose skill
I count more than upon my own. We shall be very
unfortunate if, with the weather we are having, we
do not succeed."

"The fact is," said Madame, "that there could
not be finer weather; and if you, Marquis, will permit
me to offer a suggestion, and since you are thinking
of paying the Saint-Aignans a visit, I would advise
you by all means to take advantage of the opportunity to ride over to the *Mas Brun*. I suppose you
will not be frightened at the idea, dear child," she
added, addressing Renée; "there is not a *ferrade*
every day, you know."

"I shall be delighted, Madame, especially if Germaine can come with us."

"Ah, to-morrow I cannot promise you Germaine;
I shall need her all day, and that is one reason I suggested this visit, because I am afraid you will find it
very lonely here without her."

"But, father, if you have not really decided upon
to-morrow, we can put off our visit till Germaine is
free."

" But what will you do alone most of the day, my dear ? "

" I will wander about in the neighborhood, Madame, or read and write."

" A couple of hours' ride along the Valcarès will do you a great deal more good, fair lady," interrupted the Commander, who saw that the Marquis was already wavering.

" I will be your guide, if you will allow me," cried Frederic.

" No, no," said Renée, laughing, " you promised me the bustard for to-morrow evening, and I will keep you to your word; besides, as long as we follow the Valcarès it is impossible to lose our way."

From the moment that Renée herself entered into the conspiracy the Marquis lost hope, and made up his mind to make the best of an affair from which he saw no means of escape. He spent the rest of the day in a state of feverish suspense. The night was still worse; he vainly tried to sleep, that he might forget; but scarcely did he close his eyes than the words of the abbess would ring in his ears:

" If you dispute her with God, He can take her from you."

And yet he had not strength to give her up. This interior struggle lasted all night; he would fain have put off the test, but he had gone too far to draw back now. In the morning he tried to stir himself up.

" *Cornebleu !* " said he, " it is really too absurd
that the Marquis de Blésignan, who commanded His
Majesty's gendarmes and faced the cannon a score
of times, cannot make his own daughter obey him,
any more than if he were a little tradesman. M. de
Marcoiran will be a splendid husband for her. I am
her father; she shall marry him, and he shall be my
son-in-law. *Cornebleu !* if it distresses the abbess of
St. Praxeda, let her look for consolation somewhere
else, *cornebleu !* that is all."

This heroic resolve flattered his vanity. He went
out of his room and downstairs to show M. de Forton that he was a man who was determined to act
energetically. Unfortunately he met Renée on the
stairs. She was going out to Mass. She looked at
him with her gentle, affectionate glance, said a few
words, and kissed his hand respectfully. His indomitable resolve was shaken at once. Furious with
himself, he went back to his room, saying: " I can
never speak to her." He could have beaten himself,
so angry was he at his own weakness. Breakfast-
hour came; never was the sky more pleasantly clouded
over, never was Renée gayer.

" Frederic will have a splendid day for shooting,"
said Germaine; " it is not too hot, there will be a sea-
breeze, and you will have glorious weather for your
ride."

Breakfast over, they all spent an hour or so together. The Commander related various anecdotes

in his very best style, and he was just in the midst
of an adventure upon the sea, of which he had been
the hero, when Thérésine came to say that the horses
were waiting.   The two friends exchanged an *au
revoir*, and, refusing to take any guardian with them,
arguing that they had only to keep the river in sight,
the Marquis and his daughter set off.

They at first turned to the right, riding along by
the river; but in about half an hour, wearied by the
mosquitoes, which swarmed near the water and tor-
mented their horses, they diverged in the direction
of the great rush-beds, where Renée wanted to gather
some flowers she had seen in a previous ride.   As
this field seemed near at hand and as they still kept
the Valcarès in sight, the Marquis, who had not yet
found courage to broach the all-important question,
made no objection to his daughter's wish.

" Some of those yellow daisies, which they call
fleurs d'amour," * said Renée; "with some branches
of red saltwort, and clusters of tamarisk, will be a
beautiful decoration for the altar of Notre Dame
d'Amour."

" Why, I really think you are beginning to like
Camargue," said her father.

" It is a lovely country, very curious and quite
delightful," said Renée.

" The Marcoirans are very agreeable, too."

---

* Love-flowers.

" Charming, kind, unaffected, witty, amiable, and lively."

" Do you really like them ? "

" I would be hard to please if I did not."

" Madame and her daughter are very superior people; and my friend the Commander is a thoroughly well-bred man."

" And an interesting talker," said Renée.

" The Chevalier is a fine fellow, too."

" Yes; gay, clever, and of a splendid disposition, which, as Germaine says, is always the same."

" His wife will be a fortunate woman," said the Marquis, as if talking to himself.

" Oh, indeed, I think she will," said Renée, innocently.

Just then the tinkle of a bell caused them to turn their heads. It was Ourias, who came at a gallop, followed by his tame bull, a superb beast with long horns, which he called *Ralliement*. As he passed them, the guardian called out something in a rude, imperious voice, pointing to the *Mas Rouge;* he then pursued his way across the meadows, looking from right to left, and finally, turning to the left, rode on towards a distant pine-grove.

" Decidedly, that half-savage guardian keeps spite against us for his defeat in the late *ferrade*," said Renée, smiling.

" To the devil with the blockhead ! " thought the Marquis; " I was master of the situation, and now I must dig again to reach the fortress and begin the assault."

They were quite close to the rush-bed, when, through a rent in the clouds, a shower of rays from the scorching sun fell upon the dazzling Sansouire, and suddenly illumined the plain, already much heated during the preceding days. The effect produced was so singular, the transformation so complete, that involuntarily the travellers stopped to observe it.

" Oh, what an extraordinary thing ! " said Renée. " I never remarked that lake before."

" What lake do you mean ? "

" This one, of course," said she, pointing out to her father a large blue and mirror-like surface, on the banks of which, through a grove of tall trees, could be seen a yellowish rock, surmounted by a church.

The Marquis was dumfounded.

" Les Saintes ! " cried he. " Why, that is les Saintes! There are the church, the sea, and the fishing-boats."

" Impossible ! " cried Renée; " and the proof is that here is the Valcarès, and yonder the *Château Rouge*—and yet that is les Saintes, for I recognize it too."

" Why, it is a mirage ! " cried the Marquis, all at once. " The Commander told me that such phenomena are not infrequent here during the warm weather; but certainly it is not very easy to find

one's way in a country where changes like this
occur.''

"I often heard of mirages," said Renée, "but I
thought they were only some vague, misty, fleeting
images, like the cloud-palaces, that rise and crumble
away again in the heavens, twenty times in the course
of an hour.''

"The fact is, this mirage is as clear as reality; it
is incredible that our eyes could so deceive us.''

"Let us go nearer, to see at what distance it van-
ishes," said Renée.

They galloped in its direction; but without losing
anything of its clearness, it receded as they approached. So curious were they that they spurred on
their horses without perceiving that they had gone a
considerable distance. Suddenly town, rock, and sea
disappeared like a candle blown out; the sun's rays
suddenly overclouded, their effect was at an end.
Then only did the riders perceive how far they had
gone, and turned their white horses back toward the
rush-beds, for they could no longer see the Valcarès.

"It is an ill wind that brings us no good," thought
the Marquis; "here, at least, we will not be interrupted." And he turned the conversation back to
the Marcoirans.

Renée's mind was so far from any thought of set-
tling in Camargue that to a very transparent question of her father's she replied:

"I am the better pleased to have come now, because I would probably never have seen Camargue, for there is not much likelihood that I shall ever return here."

"Unless we settle here for good and all," said her father.

Renée laughed.

"Were you thinking of transporting your château of Nyons here?" she asked.

"If you were settled here, it would suffice to transport ourselves," said her father, gravely.

He said this in such a way that Renée regarded him with some anxiety.

"I do not understand," she said.

"I mean," said he, "that if you were to marry here—to marry the Chevalier, for instance."

"I marry?" she cried. "Oh, father, do not speak of such a thing; you know very well it is not my vocation."

"A young girl's vocation is to obey her parents; I do not believe in any other," said the Marquis.

"Yet if something tells me here," said Renée, laying her hand upon her heart, "that I should consecrate myself to God, must I not obey my conscience?"

"And do you think, Mademoiselle, that this something, which is merely the effect of convent nonsense, should cause you to dispute your father's will?"

Renée was not accustomed to such severity from

her father; she hung her head, and large tears gathered in her eyes.

The Marquis grew more determined as he talked. He continued, with a calmness belied by the trembling of his voice:

"I do not know what the intentions of M. Frederic de Marcoiran's relatives may be; but if, as it may happen, they do me the honor to ask your hand, I warn you that, in spite of the absurdities with which the abbess at St. Praxeda has filled your head, I shall consider it my duty to accept so advantageous a proposal."

Renée's heart swelled. It was the first time she had ever been spoken to in such a manner.

"Do you understand?" said the Marquis, in a tone of still greater severity.

She looked at him with an expression of sorrowful submission, and answered:

"If such are your positive commands, father, I will obey them. I would rather my life should be unhappy than that I should disobey you. But remember what I tell you, that you will bring down misfortune upon us by thus opposing the designs of Providence."

These simple words made him shudder. He felt a certain hesitation, perhaps even remorse, but self-love was stronger.

Meanwhile they were fearfully anxious at the *Mas Rouge*. Frederic was returning more than an hour earlier than he had expected, when, at some distance from the château, he met Jean de l'Ourse, who said to him:

"Beware, Monsieur le Chevalier, that bad herdsman Ourias has let the *Etoile du Soir*, the bull which I marked, escape; he is looking for him everywhere in the Sansouire. It would not be safe to meet him."

"Thank you," said the officer; "but Marius and I will have our guns loaded, and if the bull appears, we will receive him in good style."

Then he went on, thinking no more of the news, because he supposed that every one was safe in the house. The first person he met was the Commander, who was anxiously awaiting his friend's return.

"I have brought back two splendid bustards," said the young officer, "and I am going to present them to Mlle. de Blésignan. I hope she will be satisfied that I have kept my promise."

"Well done!" said M. de Forton, "and I am sure that charming young lady will be very much pleased when she returns."

"Why, has she gone out?"

"Some hours ago."

"In what direction?" inquired the young officer, turning pale.

"To the *Mas Brun* with her father; you remember they were to go. I am surprised they are not back yet."

" Then they will have to cross the Sansouire. God of heaven! who is with her ?''

" Her father.''

" Only her father ?''

" Certainly; what is astonishing in that ?''

" Nothing but that the *Etoile du Soir*, the fiercest of all the Saint-Aignans' bulls, has escaped; they are looking for him in the plain. But if by chance our friends meet him, they are lost.''

This news fell like a thunderbolt. The Commander blew the horn; the guardians mounted hastily, and rode off in all directions in search of the travellers. Marius was about to ride haphazard like the rest, when a sudden thought occurred to Germaine.

" Let us go up to the balcony,'' she said; " we may see them with the glass, so that you can go straight in their direction.''

Her brother and she rushed up. They at first scanned the banks of the Valcarès, then the fields; when they came at last to the Sansouire, Frederic descried the father and daughter in the distance, riding towards the Petit-Patis. He rushed down again. When he reached the court, he found Marius on horseback, spear in hand, and with him an old *doundaire*, or tame bull, which followed him like a dog.

" To the Petit-Patis !'' he cried, jumping on a horse. " Thérésine, give me my gun.''

And they set off like a whirlwind.

Saddened by his melancholy victory, the Marquis rode silently beside his daughter, who was still weeping. When they came close to the rushes, whence they could perceive the Valcarès, the Marquis stopped a moment to ascertain their whereabouts, and, anxious to shorten the way, plunged among the sedges. He had gone about fifty paces, when his horse, shying suddenly, made so sudden a bound that it threw him, excellent rider as he was, ten paces forward on the ground. Renée, who remained in the saddle, uttered a cry of terror at sight of a black monster that arose with a frightened bellow, looked at her fiercely, his hide bristling and his hoofs pawing the sand, ready to rush upon her.

" Fly, fly, my daughter! " cried her father, whose horse, having got rid of its rider, was already far in the distance, with the stirrups flapping against his sides.

Paralyzed with terror, Renée felt herself incapable of any effort, she alternately regarding her wounded father and the bull, whose fiery nostrils were dilating with fury. She would have been lost, had not her terrified horse, disregarding spur and bridle, leaped aside to avoid the charge of his terrible enemy, and made straight for the open plain, pursued by the bull, who was foaming with rage. Renée managed to cling on to her horse, but turning her head ever and anon, saw through the whirlwind of dust raised by their mad career the fiery eyes and threatening horns of the monster, the scar of whose wound shone out from his ebony skin, like the white cross on a pall. Far, far behind this whirlwind, bareheaded, his face covered with blood, came the Marquis, never stopping to think of the utter impossibility of catching up with them in their furious course, wherein they seemed to blend in a confused mass.

Gradually the horse's strength began to fail, and the distance between him and his pursuer was momentarily diminishing. The monster's fiery breath was already upon him. Guided by instinct, he leaped aside and let the bull pass. The monster, carried on by his speed no less than by his bulk, could not turn quickly enough to pierce the fugitive's side with his horns. Astonished, and more furious than ever, the bull gave a roar and, also turning back, rushed upon the pony. This time the pursuer and pursued were speeding in the direction of the unhappy father, who, breathless from running, unarmed, and unable to find even a pebble, yet anxious to save his daughter at all hazards, did not hesitate to throw himself before the furious beast. But the latter, disdaining a foe whom his first shock rolled over in the dust, plunged into the sedges after the exhausted and panting steed. As he got up, M. de Blésignan saw the horse fall, and heard Renée's cry of horror. Then, in his despair, he fell upon his knees and cried out:

"My God! do not take her from me. I give her to Thee!"

Just then a musket-shot was heard, and the iron spear of a guardian was uplifted in the air. Riding at full speed, Marius and the Chevalier reached the spot, just as the bull, in its blind fury, had attacked the horse, butting it with his horns, and trampling upon it in his rage, close by where Renée lay in a swoon.

At the approach of these new enemies, the *Etoile du Soir*, raising his bloody head, was about to rush upon them, when the ball of the young dragoon struck him in the forehead, at the same moment that the spear of the guardian pierced his hide. This double attack would not, however, have had much effect if, just then, the tinkle of the bell and the sight of the *doundaire* had not produced its usual effect, and changed the fury of the *palusin* into docile timidity. He went over and stood beside the tame bull in the most amicable way.

Without taking any further notice of the vanquished, Frederic and Marius alighted to attend to Renée, whom they at first thought dead, but who, by a special intervention of Providence, had not received a single scratch. She had just opened her eyes, and looked round her in bewilderment, like one awaking from a dream, when her father arrived and took her in his arms. He was half-crazed with mingled joy and sorrow. He pressed her to his heart without a word; he was deadly pale, and looked as if his heart would break. He embraced Frederic and

Marius, and would fain have embraced the *doundaire* browsing quietly near his prisoner, who had lain down, panting and foaming, at his side.

From the condition of both father and daughter, it would have been impossible for them to go home on horseback, so Frederic rode off to bring a carriage, leaving them under the care of Marius. In half an hour the young officer was back; he found the hero and heroine of the drama almost entirely recovered from their emotion. Renée was calm, but her father spoke with extraordinary volubility. He took the dragoon in his arms, and whispered excitedly:

" She shall be a nun! she shall be a nun! I have sworn it. Yes, she shall be a nun !''

The Chevalier had no objection to offer; he had never thought of marrying Renée, indeed he had not thought of marrying any one; so he merely answered:

" It is a noble vocation.''

He was much more anxious just then for the arrival of the carriage, which came at length with Madame and Germaine.

" She is going to be a nun," repeated the Marquis to them.

Germaine pressed her friend's hand.

" I know that was your great desire," said she. " I congratulate you on having won your father's consent, and I will go and see you at the convent.''

Neither Madame de Marcoiran nor her brother had expected this; but Madame was a true Christian, and resigned herself with a sigh. The Commander took what he called his friend's weakness in very bad part, but hid his disappointment, partly out of politeness to his guests and partly so as not to complicate matters.

Next morning the Abbé Boucarut celebrated a Mass of Thanksgiving at Notre Dame d'Amour, at which the whole household assisted; even old Bernard came thither, leaning on his daughter's arm.

"Well, old boy," said Frederic, "what have you to say of your son-in-law now?"

"It was wrong of me to suspect him," said he, passing the back of his hard hand across his eyes to wipe away a tear of joy; "he was worthy of my daughter; he is a brave lad!"

Two days after, on his return from Arles, whither he had gone to escort the Marquis and his daughter, Frederic met Thérésine.

"Is it true," she asked, "as some say, that this lovely young lady is soon to enter the convent?"

"I believe it is certain," he answered.

"What a pity she did not come to settle in Camargue! We all hoped she would."

"But why in Camargue?"

"Because we thought she would marry her young kinsman."

"What young kinsman?"

" Monsieur Frederic de Marcoiran," said Thérésine, looking full at him.

" What nonsense ! " cried he. " It is all very well for you to marry, but I prefer my liberty. Now that we are left to ourselves, you will see what splendid shooting I shall have with your husband."

" Surely they would have made a splendid couple," said old Bernard. " Monsieur Frederic did wrong to let her slip through his fingers; he will find it hard to get such another."

Old Zounet and all the household were of the same opinion, whereas the Commander was simply furious at his friend, though he did not even then despair.

" We will settle it yet," he said to his sister, who had not the slightest hope.

One day, about three months after their departure, a messenger brought a crested letter to the Commandery, where Madame was staying. M. de Forton broke the seal, read the letter, frowned, and passed it on to his sister.

M. de Blésignan informed him of the entrance of Renée as a postulant in the Trinitarians of Bolêne, of which his cousin, Madame de Lafare, was abbess.

" It was her vocation," wrote the Marquis, " and I could not gain her consent to my most cherished wish."

" Hers was a noble soul and a rarely fine nature," sighed the widow.

The Commander shrugged his shoulders impatiently.

"Say, rather, that her father is a dotard," said he; "but there is no harm done; she has not taken any vows yet."

Early in the following month, on the very eve of a grand duck-shooting, for in autumn hundreds of these aquatic fowl gather upon the Valcarès, a corporal from Arles brought Frederic a document from the War Office. It was an order from M. de Thémine, his colonel, to rejoin his regiment in Versailles at once. Certain troubles had broken out in Paris; all the officers were recalled. He set out with swelling heart, taking leave of his people with an emotion which he himself could not explain. It seemed as if a secret presentiment warned him that he was never more to see them as they were then in his dear Camargue, where he left them at the call of duty.

CHAPTER X.

'93·

FIVE years had rolled away since the departure of the Chevalier; terrible years, each one marked by murder, revolt, incendiarism, bankruptcy, and the last by the most fearful inundation of crime that ever disgraced one of those great upheavings of a nation which history records with horror in her gloomiest annals under the name of Revolution.

The year '93 had just begun. The ancient order of things was crumbling away under the irresistible blast of the democratic tempest; the throne of the ancient monarchy and the altars raised in honor of the "Christ Who loves the Francs," were reduced to ruins. The churches were deprived of God, and the palace of Versailles was in mourning for its kings. Toulon, Lyons, Verdun fell under the hammer of the destroyers. Carrier terrified Nantes by his fierce republicanism; the army of the Convention carried fire and sword into La Vendée; priests and nobles were tracked like wild beasts by infamous informers in the pay of the Dantons, the Robespièrres, the Saint-

Justs, and other monsters, whose names are synony-
mous with scenes of horror and with the extreme of
ruffianism, fell under the daggers of the murderers,
under the blade of the guillotine, or were left to rot
on dunghills.   In the desecrated churches, apostate
priests offered their impure incense to the impure
goddess of Reason, and mingled their sacrilegious
ceremonies with the wild dances, accompanied by
the hideous *Carmagnole* or the infamous " *Ça ira.*" *

Europe, in consternation at the spectacle of these
wild beasts at first uniting for the destruction of their
victims and afterwards tearing each other to pieces,
sent its armies in all haste to form a sanitary cordon
around this fiery furnace, the flames whereof threat
ened to ignite the world.

Thus threatened with foreign invasion, the Convention, far from being intimidated, replied by the
grossest insults, and whilst it sent all the soldiers it
could collect to the frontiers, it doubled its proconsuls,
its spies, and its murderers in the interior.   Sustained
only by the terror which its audacity inspired, and
weighing upon what had been France, but what they
now called only " the Nation," that terrible régime
obtained the sinister name, which has ever since remained with it, of the " Reign of Terror."   Terror
was, in fact, the predominant feeling everywhere—in
the most remote country-places no less than in the

* *Carmagnole* and *Ça ira*, revolutionary songs.

large cities, in the midst of the agricultural population as in the great industrial centres.

" Audacity ! always audacity ! " said one of those
demoniacs in the *bonnet rouge*, beneath whose scourge
the wrath of God had forced guilty France to bow,
and who proved their power by making all good men
tremble. The Convention and its emissaries, after
having heaped insult and ignominy upon the royal
family, sent Louis the Just, the descendant of Henry
IV., Philip Augustus, and St. Louis, to the scaffold.
On the 21st January, 1793, the head of the good
king fell under the knife, on the square of the Revolution, whilst his pure soul, delivered from its long
captivity, ascended to heaven, where it besought the
offended Majesty of God to have pity on the frenzied
people. But this was not sufficient; crime must be
heaped on crime, till the cup overflowed.

Fouquier-Tinville and his worthy acolytes redoubled
their cruelty; the revolutionary tribunals forced
France to drink the chalice to the dregs. Night and
day the murderous judges, sitting in their dens, sent
suspects in cartloads to the national guillotine. The
executioners had not a moment's rest. These ministers of death gave the blood no time to cool on the
red planks, and naught was heard but the dismal
rumbling of the fatal cart, depositing its load of victims at the foot of the scaffold, or returning to the
over-crowded prisons, seeking a new cargo. In course
of time they added to the royalists those patriots

of the day before, the reactionaries of the day after, the Girondists, who had voted for the King's death more through fear than through conviction. They were nevertheless accused of moderatism, and their cowardice did not save their heads; they rolled in the dust with that of Madame Roland, the insulter of Marie-Antoinette; with that of Danton, the fierce Montagnard; with Hébert, of infamous memory; witn Carrier, the proconsul, and numbers of the other real criminals, in the same place where the head of their royal victim had fallen, and where were soon to fall those of Robespièrre, Fouquier-Tinville, Henriot, and other monsters. Most of them died a coward's death, weeping over their fate and vainly seeking for pity from a populace which replied to their entreaties by insults. It could not be otherwise; such monsters are made of blood and clay.

Such was not the death of Louis XVI., nor that of his noble and royal wife, Marie-Antoinette, Queen of France; she was calm and majestic in presence of her murderers, and mounted the steps of the scaffold as she would have ascended the steps of a throne.

Her iniquitous judges had used every effort to make her trial and sentence a torture worse than death. The indictment, read by Fouquier-Tinville in the Assembly, was a long tissue of denunciations and infamous calumnies. Hébert's deposition was still more ignoble. The Queen made no reply. Then, wishing to humiliate and, if possible, to disgrace her, the judges asked her why she was silent. She arose, and cast a long steady look upon her enemies.

"If I do not answer," she said, "it is because nature refuses to answer such an accusation brought against a mother. I appeal to all mothers who are present."

Even the tribunes responded to this sublime cry from a deeply-injured woman by admiring plaudits. The judges hung their heads in presence of a manifestation which covered them with shame. But soon, raising them again with new fury, they condemned the woman Capet to death. Everything was arranged so that she might drink the chalice slowly to the dregs. She was put into a cart, the driver of which was told to walk his horses. An actor, the comedian Grammont, disguised as a captain of artillery, rode before the cart, waving his sword, and shouting:

"Behold the infamous Antoinette!"

Just as they reached Saint-Roch's, a swarm of ruffians caused the cart to be stopped, that they might insult their royal victim. The Queen, in deep recollection, continued to pray; she did not even hear the insults, which fell off from her, in showers of mud, upon those who uttered them. At the foot of the scaffold there was another halt; it was the last upon that sorrowful way. The daughter of Maria Theresa mounted the steps with majestic tread, with-

out either weakness or bravado; and those who saw
her upon that fatal platform might well have been
convinced that it is easier to murder a queen than to
disgrace her.   There was a moment's pause, and a
dull sound, followed by a tumultuous cry of " *Vive
la République !* " which announced that the crime was
consummated.   Marie-Antoinette had entered into
immortality.

During these troubled and sorrowful years Frederic
went only twice to the *Mas Rouge*, once for the marriage of his sister Germaine with the Baron de Mont-
blanc, the second time, alas! for the funeral of that
beloved sister.   She was carried off by a fever brought
on by the terrible news of the flight of the king, and
his arrest at Varennes.   The young officer had really
come for the baptism of his sister's first child; but
he could only pray at the grave which contained
mother and child.   His sorrow was deep and in-
tense; he would fain have remained to console his
mother, but duty called him back to that royal family,
so hapless and so deserted.   All France was in revolution.   Even in the hitherto calm and peaceful Camargue insurrectionary movements began to be felt;
the guardians became threatening, and the peasantry
talked of nothing but the divisions of land which they
had so long cultivated by the sweat of their brow.
Those of the Commandery were particularly insolent;
being nearer the Rhone, and in more direct com-

munication with the boatmen of Arles, who kept them posted on what was going on in the great cities, the hotbeds of revolt, they allowed themselves to be filled with ideas of ambition and insubordination.

Quite cured of his illusions as to the new doctrines, which he had believed were to restore the golden age in France, the Commander understood at last that the philosophy of which he had been an admirer, and the States-General from which he had expected results so marvellous, were ending in crime and disorder. If his conversion was sincere, it was late, too late; what can one man do to arrest the progress of a sea? His efforts to restore discipline and command respect from his servants failed utterly, the more so that his new overseer, hoping that there was a fortune for himself in the movement which was on foot, excited the peasants to revolt.

Frederic found his uncle discouraged, alarmed, overcome with grief, and almost with remorse, for having indulged in theories the inevitable results of which he had been unable to foresee. He in fact decided to emigrate, and offer his sword to the princes who were trying to raise an army on the frontiers, to deliver France from the odious tyranny under which she groaned.

M. de Forton would willingly have taken his nephew with him, but the young man refused; not that he regarded emigration as flight or desertion, but because his duty kept him in Paris, then the

prison of the royal family, before the murderers of
Louis and Marie-Antoinette had sent their victims to
the Temple and thence to the guillotine. He departed, bidding a last farewell to his uncle and his
mother, from whom he had obtained a reluctant
promise to leave a country where her life was constantly in danger. The noble widow had indeed decided upon such a course, less to save her life, which,
after all the afflictions that had fallen upon her, she
valued little, but to spare her absent son the daily
anguish of suspense. It was arranged that she should
set out, as soon as possible, with her brother; that
old Bernard and his son-in-law should still manage
the two estates, while Thérésine should look after
the household.

On the day of Frederic's departure for Paris, Bernard accompanied his young master as far as Arles;
the wind was cold, the sky dull and lowering. Their
horses started a flock of ducks which, after circling a
moment in the air, dropped into the Valcarès. Al
most at the same moment the report of a gun made
them turn their heads. A light boat, rowed by a
vigorous oarsman, darted just then from among the
rushes, and proceeded towards the spot where the
wounded ducks had fallen.

"It is Marius," said Frederic, with a sad smile;
"yesterday evening he excused himself from coming
with me to Arles, on the plea that important business
required his presence at Aigues-Mortes."

" Hound ! " growled Bernard, clenching his fist;
" the bone-setter was right: all foundlings—"

" Do not talk like that, my dear old boy," said
Frederic. " Your son-in-law is better than you think.
Remember that his courage saved Mlle. de Blési-
gnan's life."

" I do not say to the contrary, Monsieur le Chevalier," said Bernard; " he behaved well that day, I
admit. But why did he not come to escort you,
as it was his duty to do ? "

" He is a sportsman first of all," said Frederic.
" The ducks tempted him to use his gun; he could
not resist."

" In such times as these ducks are of little importance, and especially on the day when our good master is leaving us, perhaps forever."

" Forever ? Oh, no ! I guarantee we shall hunt
together yet upon the Valcarès. I promise you, on
the word of a gentleman; that is, if I am not killed,
and if you do not desert the estate."

" God hear you and preserve you, Monsieur le
Chevalier! but as to my deserting the estate, these
rascals will never make me betray my duty; they
shall cut me into pieces before I let them pillage
your *Mas Rouge*."

" But if you should be killed too ? "

" Thérésine will be here to defend your property."

" The estate is not worth the price of such good
blood, old comrade," said Frederic: " and I hope

that once my mother and uncle are gone, no one
will dream of seizing upon property which the patriots
will believe to be in your possession."

"Thanks for your confidence, Monsieur Frederic,"
cried Bernard, passing his horny hand across his
eyes. "May God go with you and protect you!
Do not be uneasy about the *Mas Rouge;* whatever
hour of the day or night you return there, you will
always find Bernard or his daughter, and it will be
home."

At Arles there was a noisy crowd in the Place des
Hommes, all excited by the tidings of the latest
events in Paris; groups of sinister-looking men, the
very dregs of society, such as in troublous times
mount to the surface, danced the *Carmagnole,** waving their red caps and shouting the *Ça ira.*

As soon as Frederic appeared, they began to hurl
insulting epithets at him, and cry out:

"To the lantern † with aristocrats!"

Frederic grew pale with anger; he urged his horse
into the very midst of the enemy.

"Down with the defender of the tyrant!" cried a
drunken voice.

And a patriot laid a hand on the bridle of the
horse to stop it. But the Queen's Dragoon was not
one to suffer such an insult; his whip waved in the

---

* A name applied to a revolutionary dance, as well as to a song.
† In allusion to the practice of suspending aristocrats from the
street lamps or lanterns.

air and fell across the face of the insolent drunken wretch, making a bloody stripe.

"To the Rhone with the noble! to the water with the aristocrat!" cried twenty voices.

"On your knees, and ask pardon of the Nation!" repeated the guardian Ourias, the man in the red cap, who, half blinded by blood, still kept his hold of the bridle, and with his bull-strength tried to drag Frederic from his horse.

The circle closed in. The young man seemed inevitably lost, for this brutal giant would hear no reason; the multitude was thoroughly roused. There was not a moment to be lost.

"Monsieur le Chevalier," whispered Bernard, pressing close to his master, "be ready to ride off, without giving me a thought."

Then bending over to the guardian, he said:

"Ourias, you know me. I give you warning. Off with your claws, or I will knock you down."

"Death to the aristocrats!" foamed the giant.

"Will you let go?"

"Death to—"

The dull sound of the old huntsman's club was heard upon the guardian's head, and he fell his whole length upon the ground. Before the spectators had recovered from their surprise, three or four patriots were rolling in the dust, under the hoofs of the flying horses. Some pistol-shots sent after the fugitives only accelerated their speed, and in less than three minutes they were galloping along the dusty road from Arles to Avignon. No one seemed to think of pursuing them. They slackened their pace. Frederic then earnestly thanked his old friend for his interference, which had saved his life.

"It is true I had that happiness this time," answered Bernard, "but I must leave you at Beaucaire, just when you are beginning a long journey, where you will probably meet with many such adventures. Now, Monsieur Frederic, you say that you do not know how to thank me; grant me one favor, the only one which I will ask of you, and which is more than I deserve. Will you grant it?"

"On the faith of a gentleman. You have only to mention it, my friend; I promise in advance to grant it."

"Well, I beg of you, when you reach Beaucaire, to change your uniform for a civilian's dress."

"But that would be cowardice."

"No, Monsieur Frederic, only prudence. You are going to give your sword to our beloved king; your duty is, therefore, to take care of your life for his sake, and then think of your good mother, already so afflicted. Would you make her die of grief?"

"I have promised, and I will keep my promise, brave heart that you are!" cried the young man, touched by the old man's words. "Tell my mother to rest content; that I will travel in disguise, that I will meddle in no dispute, and that it is to your good advice these prudent resolutions are owing.''

'' Thanks, Monsieur le Chevalier; may God reward your goodness to an old servant who, come what may, will be always faithful to you ! ''

They continued to ride on, conversing of many things, and discussing the precautions to be taken for Madame de Marcoiran's flight. Bernard and Thérésine were to accompany her, together with the Commander, under pretence of a pilgrimage to les Saintes, as far as Aigues-Mortes, where they would secretly embark for Spain on one of those little merchant-vessels which trade between that port and Barcelona.

When they reached Beaucaire they exchanged their last greetings and mutual recommendations. The Chevalier having again promised his foster-father to return and shoot ducks with him on the Valcarès, they parted, the old huntsman cutting across country towards Saint-Gilles, and the Queen's Dragoon, disguised as a merchant travelling on business, rode on to Rogonas, to take the ferryboat across the river of la Durance, which forms the boundary on that side of the county of Venaissin. Bernard returned unobserved.

It was not until some days later that the news spread through the country of the Chevalier's encounter at Arles, and of the death of Ourias, which occurred the day after he had been struck by Bernard's club.

Such an event made but a slight sensation at that time; the law took little cognizance of such matters, especially as Ourias had been a sort of bandit, both feared and hated.

Marius, who had foreseen in him a future rival, and against whom the guardian had cherished a deadly hatred, would certainly have been rejoiced had he not feared that his father-in-law's intervention in favor of the Chevalier might militate against him and his own designs. For there was already talk of confiscating the goods of *émigrés* or of those who had fallen under the justice of the people, and though too crafty to make known his real sentiments to his wife or father-in-law, Marius was speculating upon a near future, and wishing with all his heart for the triumph of the revolution, which would, he hoped, humble his former masters and enrich himself.

Thérésine never suspected her husband's baseness, and she was convinced that he would be, like herself and her father, rejoiced when, about three weeks after Frederic's departure, a letter came from him, addressed to Madame de Marcoiran, announcing his safe arrival in Paris.

"Poor dear Chevalier!" cried Bernard, "he is not out of danger yet, but in Paris he is at least not alone; and with so many others he may be useful to the King and Queen, and, sword in hand, help to drive back the brigands who dare to attack them."

"I do not think things are as bad as they are

generally reported," said Marius; "troubles like
these are always exaggerated at a distance, and when
there is a disturbance as big as my finger it is said
to be as big as my arm."

"Nevertheless Monsieur Frederic was near being
thrown into the Rhone," cried Bernard.

"I should think so, with that brute of an Ourias;
he wanted to meddle in everything, and you did well
to rid the country of him."

"I am sorry I killed him, but he forced me to do
it," sighed Bernard. "I had no wish to get rid of
him."

"Bah!" cried Marius, "dead men do not bite.
He might have done harm, and he was our deadly
enemy."

"We should pardon our enemies and not kill
them," said Thérésine; "life is in God's hand, and
rash is he who dares to send before its Judge a soul
made to the image of the Creator."

Marius was not of this opinion. Ourias had been
a weight on his mind, and he felt that his father-in-
law had done him a good turn in ridding him of an
obstacle which might at any given moment become
dangerous.

Events succeeded each other with fearful rapidity.
The commotions which deluged the large towns with
blood found an echo in the provinces; almost every
week brought news that the peasants had arisen, and
murdered some lord or burned some castle.

The Saint-Aignans were obliged to leave the *Mas Brun* in consequence of a revolt of their guardians. Those of the Commandery became more and more insolent every day. M. de Forton saw that the time had come for him to hasten to the army of the princes, returning with it to chastise the rebels that were spreading fire and blood through the Kingdom of the Lilies. Once convinced of this he wrote to his old companion-at-arms proposing that he should go with them into Spain or Germany, where numbers of *émigrés* were assembled.

M. de Blésignan answered:

"*Monsieur and much-honored Friend :* I thank you for your kind attention, but I have long since sworn that these rascals, these robbers, these ruffians, who only await our departure to seize upon our goods, shall never see my heels. I will not do them the honor to leave my castle. If they wish to pillage it, let them come; I will receive them in good style. *Cornebleu !* it will cost them dear to hang the corpse of the Seigneur of Nyons to a lantern. To-day my Renée was professed, and took the veil in the Convent of the Trinitarians. My life is no longer necessary to any one; I look forward but to one pleasure in life, and of that I shall certainly not deprive myself. It is to teach these brigands of patriots, these red-capped robbers and cutthroats, a lesson which they will not forget.

"You have my most heart-felt wishes for the safe

issue of your journey and that of the most honored
Madame de Marcoiran; but I repeat, my mind is
made up. The Marquis de Blésignan will die, if
needs be, but die like his ancestors, in armor, sword
in hand, his face towards the foe.

" Upon which, I pray God, Monsieur, and much-
honored friend, that He may keep you in His holy
care.

" Vive Dieu ! Long live the King !
    " GUILLAUME, *Marquis de Blésignan.*'

" He is very wrong, but he has a noble heart,"
said the Commander, after having read this letter to
his sister. " I know him well; it is useless to insist."
Three days after, at dawn of day, four horses set out
from the *Mas Rouge* for Aigues-Mortes, and, passing
through the town, arrived the same evening at Grau-du-
Roi, a little village composed of some twenty thatched
cabins, skirting the canal. Under one of these thatch-
covered roofs, in company with several brave sailors,
Madame de Marcoiran spent this last night. The
next day the Commander and she, taking with them
all the money and jewels which, thanks to Bernard,
they had been able to gather together, embarked on
a Spanish vessel bound for Barcelona. Thérésine
burst into tears; Bernard wept also. Madame de
Marcoiran embraced Thérésine, and gave her hand
to the old huntsman to kiss, saying:
    " I confide to you the property of my son and

the grave of my daughter. I know that I can depend on your courage and fidelity.''

'' We will soon return,'' said the Commander, '' do
not fear. God will never permit injustice and revolt
to triumph over justice and right.''

M. de Forton believed his words prophetic, but,
alas! he was grievously mistaken.

The wrath of Heaven demanded a longer and more
terrible expiation. Streams of innocent blood must
inundate guilty France, to purify it from the blas-
phemies uttered against God by the philosophers,
from the spirit of irreligion which had seized upon
the nobility, and the scandal given to the world by
royalty in the reign of Louis XV. The Revolution,
unchained by the States-General, continued to advance with giant strides.

On the 20th of June, 1792, the wretches who had
already invaded Versailles, and applauded the entrance of Louis XVI. into Paris, after his arrest at
Varennes, now poured like a torrent into the palace
of the Tuileries, massacred the faithful guards, penetrated the royal apartments, and forced an entrance
into the presence of the Queen.

This new insult, remaining unpunished, was a fresh
incentive to the populace, who felt themselves masters of the situation. Wholly without restraint,
they stopped at nothing. The manifesto by which
the Duke of Brunswick declared, in the name of the
coalition of kings, that he would invade France, re-

store Louis XVI. to his rights and France to order, only roused the populace to new fury, and urged them on to fresh excesses. On the 10th of August the palace was attacked for the second time. The Swiss Guards defended it bravely; but the King, to save bloodshed, commanded them to cease firing. This was the signal for the massacre of these brave men by monsters drunk with wine and fury. On the 2d of September a still more atrocious crime, the massacre of the prisoners in the abbey, was commanded in cold blood by Danton.

Maillard and his cutthroats, in the pay of the new republican government, devoted themselves for three whole days to the massacre of the suspects brought to them in loaded carts called provision-baskets. Blood flowed in torrents. The Carmes had its turn after the abbey, and there numbers of priests were massacred.

These terrible crimes, which inaugurated the era of assassinations, were followed by no less terrible crimes in the provinces.

At Camargue the guardians of the Baron de Saint-Aignan set the example by burning the *Mas Brun;* those of the Commandery contented themselves with dividing the property of M. de Forton, which was cut up into shares. Bernard, threatened with death by the pillagers, found it impossible to stay the progress of events or make the spoilers relinquish their prey.

At *Maison Rouge* things were not so bad; the guardians, ever kindly treated by Madame de Marcoiran, remained faithful to their former lord. On the whole estate there were scarcely two or three who ventured to speak of imitating their neighbors at the Commandery. Marius, to the great satisfaction of his father-in-law, who continued to distrust him, received these suggestions very ill; he showed the rebellious that he was a master who would not allow himself to be intimidated, and immediately drove them from the domain. This summary proceeding sufficed to restore order, which was not again disturbed.

The year passed thus. '93, of sinister memory, dawned; fatal year, ushered in by the regicide of the 21st January, which disgraced France in the eyes of the whole civilized world, and inaugurated the Reign of Terror during which the revolutionary tribunals shed torrents of the purest and noblest blood in the kingdom. Under the knife of the guillotine fell innumerable heads. The churches were everywhere profaned, the altars overthrown, the sacred vessels desecrated; the property of monasteries, like that of the *émigrés*, sold, for a few handfuls of *assignats*,* to miserable speculators, who, through greed of gain, became accomplices of the thefts committed by the Nation.

* The paper money of the Revolution

The *Mas Rouge* was not forgotten by this brigand government, always in quest of new confiscations, always at the end of their resources, spending millions to become bankrupt.

Bernard had expected the sale of the property, and prepared for it by saving all the money that he possibly could. He dared not proceed himself to Arles, where he was too well known and where he knew that he would be at once imprisoned. But he sent Marius, who, out of prudence, or even, as he said, out of devotion to his master, had affected the most advanced opinions, joined a patriotic club, and deserved by his terrorist ideas to be made municipal officer of the Saintes-Maries, now called Montagne-Marie.

The sale by auction took place on the 16th October, the very day of the execution of Marie-Antoinette. When Marius came back in the evening he was not yet aware of this new crime; but what he did know was that he had been made by the Nation proprietor of the *Mas Rouge ;* that the lands, the flocks, the house, the garden, and a portion of the river belonged to him. It had cost him some louis d'or, some twenty-four pounds, and a handful of *assignats.* Neither Madame nor the Commander had any further rights over these estates. The Chevalier, the only one who could claim any rights of property after the Revolution, had not been heard of for a year. He had probably perished at Paris, in the siege of the castle, or had been imprisoned, in which latter case the national guillotine would soon cut short his ulterior pretensions.

Thérésine's husband came home radiant; his dream was at last realized; he, the foundling, the lad brought up on charity, the overseer liable to be dismissed any day, was now suzerain lord. He felt as if he were walking on air. Henceforth he had only one thought: to make his lands bring in as much as possible. It would be the worse for the idlers. He would be pitiless to them. The husband of old Zounet, a farmer, could not pay his rent; he would drive him thence; he would feed no idle mouths. The peasants would find out the difference between an idiotic noble and an intelligent citizen who had suddenly come into power. All this rushed into his mind at once; yet as he approached the house, he bethought himself of Thérésine and Bernard, those devotees of royalty, and a cloud passed over his face, for he remembered that his father-in-law, always distrustful, before giving him the money had made him sign a deed by which he, Marius, acknowledged that he was only acting in his father-in-law's name and as a bidder. The old man could not last long, but in the meantime he must not quarrel with him, much less let him guess his plans. Marius was, however, a complete master of the art of hypocrisy; he therefore assumed a downcast air on arriving at the farm, threw aside his cloak with an expression of the deepest grief, and, giving some papers to his father-in-law, said:

"Here are the title-deeds, but our money has all gone."

"What matter!" cried Bernard, radiant, "so long as Monsieur Frederic is sure to find his domain intact."

"We shall be ruined none the less," growled Marius.

"Bah!" said Thérésine. "The Chevalier will return us what we have advanced out of the rents."

"That reminds me," cried the overseer, seizing the opportunity, "that we must try to be more exact about the rents; we should betray his confidence were we to act otherwise."

"You are right," said Thérésine; "these revenues should be more sacred than ever to us now."

Bernard was of the same opinion; so it was agreed that Marius, in whose intelligence they had great confidence, should administer the estate so as to improve it as much as possible. This was just what Marius wanted.

"I will do for him as I would do for myself," he said; and he kept his word, for it was really for himself that he worked.

Nevertheless, he continued to be of the municipal council of les Saintes, where he posed as a furious republican and a fiery partisan of Robespièrre. Bernard was much scandalized by this affectation of *sans-*

culottism, and sometimes asked himself in affright whom Marius was really deceiving; but the latter always replied to such observations by saying:

" We must howl with the wolves if we would prevent them from devouring us. Let us, above all things, save the property of our good Monsieur Frederic."

Thérésine, who was less credulous, wept in secret; her instinct warned her that Marius was only playing a game. Yet she dared not confide her fears to her father. Bernard, hot-headed as he was, might be the cause of new misfortunes. If only she could get news of Monsieur Frederic! She knew that his name had been placed on the list of *émigrés*, and that if he were taken he would be guillotined, like all who were dragged before the revolutionary tribunals, and denounced there by traitors and ruffians. Therefore, while fully believing him to be in France, she feigned to think him in Spain or Italy. At times her suspense was torturing. Moreover, there was no chance of hearing from him. A letter from an *émigré*, intercepted at the post-office, would be a crime sufficient to send the person to whom it was addressed to the guillotine. Far less than that sufficed: a name imprudently pronounced, a gesture, a glance, and one might be denounced and imprisoned.

Amid this universal terror, which paralyzed even thought, one man, perhaps the only one in France, preserved his liberty of thought and action. This man was the Marquis de Blésignan. Instead of emigrating like his friends, he had, as he said, made his ancient castle into a fortress, and provisioned it with arms and ammunition. From behind these walls he defied the Republic. His courage was so astonishing that he might have been spared, and regarded merely as a harmless fool, had not his property tempted the cupidity of some ruffians in the vicinity of Nyons.

A shoemaker who was president of the Montagnard* club—for there were Montagnards everywhere, and clubs for all Montagnards—denounced him to the tribunal at Orange as a dangerous conspirator, who was keeping up an active correspondence with the enemies of France. Two gendarmes were sent to arrest him, but he had been warned and the gates were closed; they knocked, but no one answered. At last the Marquis appeared at a window, and asked what they wanted.

"We come to summon you, in the name of the law, to appear before the tribunal," answered one of them.

"If that is all," cried the Marquis, "you can go back, my friend. I recognize neither your law nor your tribunals. I am in my own house; let your cutthroat judges come to seek me here, if they dare."

This reply, which was an actual challenge to the Republic, produced an outburst of rage on the part

---

* A fiery republican under the Revolution.

of its myrmidons. The same evening ten gendarmes and twenty national guardsmen came from Orange and passed through Nyons, announcing that they were going to seize the ruffian and drag him in fetters to prison, from which he would come out next day to *cracher dans le panier*.* The shoemaker loudly applauded this declaration, which promised to realize his most ardent desire, and fiercely displayed a red flag—that hideous blood-colored rag, so worthy of the wretches who rallied round it, asking as an honor to be allowed himself to guide them to the castle.

The setting sun was just gilding the ancient château, when the savage troop, shouting the *Ça ira*, arrived before it. All was silent and it would almost seem deserted. The great iron-barred door was closed. The corporal knocked in the name of the law. There was no answer.

"If the old wolf will not come out, we must force our way into his den," shouted the shoemaker. "Give me an axe, and you shall see."

However, no one had an axe; so he went off with five or six patriots to procure one, as well as crowbars and other instruments. The national guardsmen amused themselves in his absence by peppering the grated windows. And meanwhile, in the small arched room which served him as an arsenal, the Marquis was coolly loading his muskets, and placing them

---

* A vulgar expression, literally to spit in the basket, meaning that the head of the Marquis would fall on the guillotine.

at windows overlooking the meadows. He had sent his faithful servant away to Lyons that morning on some pretence, so that he alone composed the garrison of his castle. When he heard the first blows of the axe upon the door, he mounted by a ladder to a narrow gun-hole, seized a two-barrelled gun, took aim with all the coolness of a hunter, and fired two shots.

At the noise of the double report, which they were so far from expecting, and at sight of their ensign-bearer and one of the gendarmes lying dead on the ground, the volunteers of the Republic, forgetting their bravery, fled in disorder, throwing their arms to the wind, falling over each other, and deaf to the voice of the corporal.

However, the gendarmes, not wishing to be associated in this ignominious flight, directed their fire towards the gun-hole, in order to give one of their comrades an opportunity to make a breach in the door. But this time the shots came from quite another direction, and the infallible bullets of the Marquis laid the hapless breachmaker low, and mortally wounded the corporal. Deprived of their leader, whom they carried off dying, the gendarmes availed themselves of the generosity of their adversary, who might have exterminated them had he so wished, and returned to the village, whence they had to send to Nyons for reinforcements, for the Montagnards absolutely refused even to remove the body of their president.

Next day, the same gendarmes, bearing a flag of truce to announce that they did not come as enemies, appeared before the walls. The Marquis addressed them from a high battlement, excusing himself for being obliged to kill soldiers whom he esteemed, but declaring that he would give no quarter. He wore the uniform of the King's household troops, with the cross of Saint Louis on his breast, and appeared with head uncovered. When he had finished speaking he returned to his donjon, whence, almost immediately, the white royalist flag was seen to float.

Regular siege had now to be laid to this feudal den, as the Republican Committee contemptuously styled it. The siege commenced by a blockade, and was continued by the establishment of batteries and the digging of trenches. Gendarmes and a company of the national guard were sent at first. But regular troops had to be summoned, and these were picked off so skilfully by the ever-invisible Marquis that at the end of a week the assailants had not advanced a step. New troops, from Orange and Pont Saint-Esprit, under the command of a regular general, Albignac, were ordered to the spot; for, incredible as it may seem, this account is perfectly historical. They arrived at length with artillery. The republican army could now cannonade from afar the solitary aristocrat, who, alone and unaided, so long kept his ground against the enemy.

At this distance his muskets were of no farther

use, but he remembered an old gun ten feet long, and bringing it forth, used it to overthrow a couple of dozen Blues. The general had the cannons moved backwards. Knowing that it was a waste of ammunition, the Marquis then ceased fire. They thought he was going to surrender.

" Down with the Republic! Long live the King ! " was his reply to the flag of truce.

The siege was becoming more and more ignominious. At last incendiary bombs were brought into play.

Cornebleu! M. de Blésignan might well have admired the stone slating on the church of les Saintes; the oak framework of his château took fire at once; he could not put it out by his own unaided efforts.

The republicans seized the opportunity to assail the gates, which did not long withstand their efforts. They were quickly forced, and the wretches rushed like an avalanche into the court, anxious to possess themselves of the person of the brigand who had killed so many patriots, and to carry away his head upon their pikes. A curtain of fire arrested their progress; the flames were spreading rapidly, pouring out through the roof and from every casement, devouring the woodwork and obstructing all the doors. Suddenly a figure was seen outlined against that red and ominous background. It was the Marquis, who appeared, bareheaded and still in full uniform, on the balcony. He held a dark object in his hands. It seemed to be a case, probably containing his papers and jewels. There was a moment of suspense; none could guess what he was going to do with it. He raised it high above his head, and threw it among the multitude below, who crowded with the greed of wild beasts round this treasure sent by the enemy.

All at once there was a loud report; a breach was made among the ravenous crew, and shrieks of mingled fear and pain echoed through the court, already strewn with bloody remnants.

" Long live the King ! cried the Marquis, waving his hand. " Long live the King ! "

The coffer which he had thrown to them contained the last of his ammunition.

" Long live the King ! " he repeated, darting in among the flames which barred his passage.

His after-fate was never known, but it would seem that he perished in the ruins of his château.

CHAPTER XI.

THE TERROR.

SEVERAL months had elapsed since the event we have related, before the news of the noble defence made by the Marquis de Blésignan, and of the infamous vengeance taken by the patriots of Nyons, arrived at the *Mas Rouge.* The insult offered to the national guard of the town exasperated the Montagnard club, the more so as the siege of the castle had served to display the cowardice of many of its members. In their rage, some of these wretches bethought themselves of the daughter of the Marquis, and resolved to vent their wrath upon her. Seeking Renée's whereabouts, they discovered that, like many other victims forgotten in the dungeons, since the guillotine could not suffice to empty them, she was with her companions in the prisons of Bolêne; then, with a savage joy, they hastened to denounce her. At this epoch, so fertile in monsters, the revolutionary tribunal of Orange had the melancholy privilege of being remarkable for the ruffianism of its members.

A summons to appear at the bar was at once brought against the imprisoned religious, and the public prosecutor prepared in advance an indictment which he expected would produce a veritable sensation, as well from the enormity of the crimes with which they were charged as by the sentimental and extravagant terms in which it was couched.

The journal brought from Arles by Marius, who had gone thither with some furious patriots to take part in one of those hideously burlesque festivals which the high-priest of Reason, the hypocritical and sentimental Robespierre, substituted for the solemnities of the Catholic Church, chronicled the arrival at Orange of the twenty-five enemies of the Republic, huddled into three carts and escorted by valiant patriots who had not hesitated to undergo the fatigue of a long journey in order that none of these wretches should escape the avenging blade of justice.

" Brought before the revolutionary tribunal, these priest-perverted women," said the republican editor, " carried their audacity so far as to deny the horrible crime of high treason, of which they were accused by trustworthy evidence. Happily, the honest judges were not deceived by these denials, and, consulting only their outraged patriotism, condemned these twenty-five criminals to the guillotine. Twelve of them underwent the final penalty amid the applause of all true patriots. The thirteen others were kept over till the next day, on account of the lateness of the hour and also because of certain criminal demonstrations on the part of a few citizens, who were touched by an unpatriotic and most censurable pity towards the accused. The prisoners, young in years, were already hardened in criminal fanaticism, of which they all, and especially the before-named Renée de Blésignan, the last guillotined, gave a striking manifestation upon the scaffold.''

'' Poor young lady!'' said Thérésine, bursting into tears, '' she was Mlle. Germaine's best friend, and an angel from heaven. These brigands of republicans only gave her back her wings when they put her to death.''

'' She died like a saint,'' said Marius; '' the journal does not tell all.''

'' All these holy women died an admirable death, of course,'' said Thérésine, '' and I am sure that the noble daughter of the Marquis de Blésignan showed as much courage and coolness as any of her companions.''

'' I gathered from an eye-witness to the execution,'' said Marius, who was anxious to appear in old Bernard's eyes all that he really was not, '' that this last crime will bring misfortune upon Robespierre. The people are beginning to be tired of all these executions, and seem to have got a surfeit of blood. They were afraid of an anti-patriotic movement, and it was not really because it was late, but because the judges were afraid of a rising among the people, that the last religious were taken back to the prison.''

'' The people are too cowardly to revolt,'' growled

Bernard, striking his forehead with his clenched fist;
"yes, too cowardly."

"Except the Vendéans," said Thérésine, with animation.

"Ah !" cried her father, "if I were twenty years
younger, M. de la Rochejacquelein * would count
another musket, and the Blues some scores of soldiers
less."

Marius said nothing, but sighed deeply.

"Yes," cried his father-in-law, "you may well
sigh!   Were I in your place, I would be there."

"I think my presence is much more useful here
than it would be in le Bocage; † you would not be
able alone to control the tenants of the *Mas Rouge*
and keep the land for its lawful owners."

"True," said Bernard, in a softened tone; and
changing the subject abruptly, said: "Tell us all
that passed in Orange."

"These holy nuns arrived there in the morning,"
said Marius, assuming a tone of emotion worthy of
the most finished actor; "they were dragged to the
tribunal, where, as you know, the judges relieve each
other, so as not to keep the guillotine waiting.
Hearing of their arrival, a great crowd hastened to
see and perhaps to insult them.   But the moment
the prisoners entered the hall, the people seemed to
change.   The nuns came in with their veils lowered,

* The Marquis de la Rochejacquelein, a leader of La Vendée.
† A district of La Vendée.

their hands crossed upon their breasts, and advanced two by two to their places in the dock, where they sat down as they used to sit in the stalls of their church. Last of all came the abbess, Madame de Lafare, a tall, majestic woman; she walked slowly, with her eyes fixed upon the ground, quite calm and undisturbed. A few shouts were heard, stifled at once. There was perfect silence in the court. This was not what the judges had expected, and it made them uneasy. On a sign from the judge, the public prosecutor rose; he counted a great deal upon the effect of what he was about to read. He began in a voice of thunder, but from the first everything went against him. His horrible charges against these poor women were ridiculous, and his most fiery outbursts were received in cold silence. So he lowered his voice, and stammered through with the indictment, finishing it up as quickly as possible.

" The trial then began. Every detail of it was just the same. All kinds of questions were put to the nuns, to make them criminate themselves, but they always answered quietly, and every one knew that what they said was true. There was not one in the court, even the worst disposed, that was not sure of their innocence, and that they had right on their side. No one had ever come into the court with a braver face than Madame de Lafare. Her answers fairly crushed the judges, and reduced their accusations to powder. The false witnesses, called to testify against the nuns, were frightened by her proud looks, and became so confused that murmurs were heard from every part of the house. The court had never seen anything like it. The judge was furious, and ordered the hall to be cleared, threatening that the first person who showed the least sign of pity for the accused would be imprisoned as a suspect. Then the drums beat and the volunteers were called out, they said to protect the Republic against the factions, but in reality to escort the religious to the guillotine; for, as soon as the hall was cleared, the judges, without much deliberation, condemned the prisoners to death. They came out as they had gone in, two by two, between a double row of brigands, armed with pikes and muskets. They were admirable, their faces lit up by faith and the hope of martyrdom. When they reached the scaffold, which was surrounded by a dense crowd of silent and agitated spectators, they raised their veils, and stood round the foot of the scaffold, to sing the Litany for the Dying. Then they knelt, one by one, before the abbess, who gave them her blessing and pointed up to heaven. The executioner and his assistants were waiting upon the scaffold. The first nun raised her veil, arranged the folds of her dress, and went up the steps. She was very young and extremely beautiful, and with a countenance so sweet that it brought tears to many eyes. When she reached the top, she clasped her hands, and knelt upon the boards, as if she were going to receive Communion. The executioner pushed her forward, the knife fell, and she had gone to heaven.

" ' Long live the Republic! Death to aristocrats ! ' cried a few voices; but these cries were not taken up, and died away in a threatening murmur. A second religious ascended the scaffold. She was an elderly woman with an energetic face; she looked round a moment, smiling and confident, raised her hands to heaven, and knelt as her companion had done, while her sisters at the foot of the scaffold still sang the Litany for the Dying.

" As each head fell, pity turned into anger. The storm was gathering. Mlle. de Blésignan's execution made it burst forth. Many of the spectators had known her; many had experienced kindness from her. When they saw her standing on the scaffold, with her pale face, her large blue eyes, so sweet and heavenly, her queenly figure, her golden hair cut short under the veil, which had been removed, there was a pause as if they were all stupefied. The Litany was just ended; the religious, who were themselves to die, sang the Te Deum over the corpses of their companions. It was a hymn of triumph in honor of the eleven virgin martyrs, whom they seemed to see soaring with green palm-branches above the blood-stained scaffold.

" ' Pardon ! pardon ! ' cried the crowd, pressing in

a threatening manner around the volunteers of the Republic.

" The executioner hesitated.

" ' Come, hurry up, and finish your work ! ' cried the commander of the escort, with a fearful oath.

" ' Pardon ! pardon ! ' ' No more executions ! ' roared the threatening crowd.   It seemed as if Mlle. Renée was afraid that the crown of martyrdom would be snatched from her.

" She looked round entreatingly, as if saying, ' Let me die for God and my religion,' and, crossing her arms, knelt down.   One of the executioners advanced; but before he could touch her, the noble daughter of the Marquis had laid her neck upon the block, the red knife gleamed, the blood gushed forth, and her beautiful head rolled into the basket.   Then the repressed rage of the spectators burst forth.   There were cries of, ' Death to the assassins ! ' on all sides. The volunteers were pushed forward to the very steps of the scaffold.   A shower of stones fell around the executioner; one of them struck the commander in the head, and threw him down covered with blood.

" Fear seized upon the brigands; they surrounded the thirteen religious who were awaiting their turn, and brought them back to prison amid shouts and curses and groans.   It was whispered that an old nun had predicted to Madame de Lafare that she should be very near death and escape it.   On her return to prison she wept that she had not followed her daughters to the tribunal of God."*

"What they did not do to-day they will do to-morrow," cried Bernard; "these monsters will not let their prey escape."

"Who knows?" said Marius. "The man who told me all this said that the guillotine had been set on fire, and the knife broken; that the volunteers had to hide, and that he would not be surprised if the Reign of Terror were nearly over. Oh, I would joyfully give my life to see the end of it."

"Well spoken, lad!" said Bernard, deeply moved by what he had heard, and perhaps even more by the profoundly Christian sentiments of Marius, whom, he now reproached himself, he had unjustly suspected.

"Yes," continued Thérésine, "these excesses fill us with horror, and I tremble lest, some day or other, we may learn that our good Monsieur Frederic has perished in the same way."

"Certainly," said Marius, "I felt great sorrow for the death of Mlle. de Blésignan, whose life I once saved with the help of our noble master; but if anything should happen to the Chevalier, I would

---

* The defence of the Castle of Blésignan is a historical fact, the proofs of which the author has in his hands; the execution of the Trinitarians at Bolène also took place under the circumstances described above. Madame de Lafare and twelve other nuns were taken back to prison, and released after the fall of Robespierre.

be inconsolable. Ah, those who think and say that I would rejoice at his death are indeed mistaken; no one is more attached to him than I. I must really love him better than myself, to disgrace myself for his sake alone, by appearing to share the opinion of these infamous republicans, whom I hold in horror."

Bernard, who was honesty itself, never doubted that these words of Marius came straight from his heart; his face fairly beamed as he arose and clasped him in his arms, saying:

"Pardon me, my son, that I have too long mistrusted you; now I more than believe in you. I am certain that you are one of ourselves, a good royalist, ready to restore his property to the Chevalier as soon as he returns."

"Restore it?" cried Marius. "Did you for a moment suppose that I considered myself anything more . than what I had always been—the overseer?"

"Then you would give up his lands to him without regret?"

"Say rather with the greatest pleasure; I would cry out to him:

"'Chevalier, we have kept guard, in your absence, at the door of your house. Here are the keys; take them back. You owe us no gratitude; we have only done our duty.'"

"Do you hear, Thérésine, do you hear?" cried the old man, weeping with joy. "And to think that I distrusted him, that for security I made him sign a paper which I confided to a notary with my will. To-morrow I will go and bring that paper here. I want you to tear it up in my presence. Do you hear, Marius ?"

" Yes, father, I hear and thank you; but I will not accept your offer. I want you to be able to say to Monsieur Frederic:

" ' It is I, your old foster-father, who redeemed your estate and now restores it to you.' "

These sentiments were so very fine that Thérésine instinctively felt them to be at least exaggerated. However, unwilling to disturb her father's happiness, and to reawaken suspicions which she was conscious of having shared, she made pretence of going upstairs to close the windows, which she always opened during the day to air the house, and left the room. It was already dark, and taking a lamp she went up to the room once occupied by her dear Germaine. The air was infinitely sweet and balmy; she went out on the balcony, where all was fragrant with the breath of many flowers which her own hands had cultivated, in memory of her whom she had so loved. Standing there her thoughts reverted to the past. The sky was frosted with many stars; the sight of it awoke a memory, and unconsciously, without knowing why, she began to sing:

" O Magali, ma tant amado,
    Mete la teste au fenestroun !
    Escouto un pau aquesto aubado
    De tambourin e de viouloun."

She remembered then how she had sung this song years before, down in the garden among the flowers, and how Frederic had replied from without the hedge.

She leaned her head sadly upon her hand. All at once she heard a light step; she quickly raised her head, and almost screamed as she perceived a figure advancing in the shadow of the wall. Thérésine was distinctly visible to any one without, because of the lamp on the table; but its light prevented her from distinguishing objects. She was about to warn her husband that there was some one prowling around the house, when a rich, sweet voice, tremulous with emotion, took up the second verse of the song:

> "Ei plen d'estello, aperamount!
> L 'auro es toumbado,
> Mai lis estèlo paliran
> Quand te veiran!"

Thérésine stood motionless, overcome with amazement; it seemed as if her heart would leap out of her breast. But the voice which had produced this effect once hushed, the charm was broken, and the Provençale, excited, beside herself, half frantic, rushed headlong downstairs and into the room where her husband and father sat, crying:

"Quick! quick! he is here! My God! have pity on him, save him!"

"What is it? what is the matter?" cried the two men, amazed at her inexplicable behavior.

But without even listening to them, she opened

the door and rushed out into the darkness. Marius
seized his gun, loaded the barrels, and followed, supposing that there were thieves in the garden. Bernard, of the same opinion, took his carabine and
loaded it. In those troublous times people were prepared for anything. He was about to go out, when
Thérésine came in fairly beaming with joy, followed
by a stranger, whose face and figure were completely
concealed by a cloak and a broad-brimmed hat. Behind his wife came Marius, musket in hand and with
threatening aspect, for he knew not with whom he
had to deal or how he was to treat the new-comer.

"Come in without fear," cried Thérésine; "there
are none here but ourselves."

Then turning to her husband, she said:

"Close the door carefully."

Still the unknown one was silent, and made no
movement towards solving the mystery. Naturally
impatient, the old huntsman snatched up a candle
from the table, and held it to the stranger's face.
He saw that it was that of a man about thirty years
of age, with fiery red hair and beard, whose throat
and chin were concealed by a muffler, while an ample
cloak covered him completely, showing only the tops
of his high boots and the end of one of those heavy
clubs which were sometimes worn only as a fashion-
able eccentricity, but which in the hands of a
determined man might easily become a terrible
weapon.

" Well, who are you, and what do you want ?" cried Marius, angrily.

" It is a sad thing to have risked one's head a hundred times for the sake of shaking hands with some old friends who do not even recognize me," cried the stranger, throwing off his hat and the red wig which concealed his black silky hair.

" Monsieur Frederic, my son !" cried Bernard, trembling violently.

" Well, old comrade, will you not embrace me ?" asked Frederic.

" Oh, my good, my dear master !" cried the old man, melting into tears and opening his arms to receive the outlaw.

Pale as death, a prey to mingled rage and despair at beholding the Chevalier under this roof, of which he had believed himself the proprietor, Marius stood gazing upon his abhorred rival, that execrable noble to whom he must now restore an inheritance which he had believed entirely his own. He trembled in every limb with uncontrollable rage, whilst his teeth chattered and a cold sweat stood out upon his forehead.

" Oh, that I had met him alone in the Sansouire," he thought, " and he would never have reached here alive!"

Rooted to the spot by his blind passion, he convulsively clasped the barrel of his gun, the while his wife and father-in-law seemed to mock him by the

eagerness with which they pressed round this fine
Chevalier, for whom he himself, a few minutes before,
had stupidly made so many professions of devotion.
How he would have liked to see that head falling
under the blade of the guillotine! What did it matter to him that so many others had fallen, since for
him the Republic, that is to say, his whole fortune,
all his ill-gotten gains, depended upon that one head.

" Will you not shake hands with me too, my dear
Marius ?" asked Frederic, turning to him.

Sullenly the patriot gave his hand.

" Come, I see that you have not forgotten my
double shot at the partridges," said the officer, smiling.

" Don't believe a word of it, Monsieur Frederic,"
said Bernard, hastily. " We were talking of you
only a few minutes ago, and he said that the happiest
day of his life would be that upon which he could
restore you your lands and your château, saying:
' Here is your property; now if you wish to keep me
as your overseer, do.' "

" Bad head and good heart, why then do you give
me so cold a greeting ?" said Frederic. " Are you
afraid I will compromise you ?"

" I am not a noble, and there is no price on my
head," said Marius, dryly and with a sinister smile.

Thérésine looked anxiously at her husband; the
expression of his face made her shudder.

" Perhaps you would like to get that price ?" said
the dragoon, jestingly.

" If not I, there are plenty of others to try for it,"
growled Marius; " and the simple fact of your presence here, were it known, would send us all to the
scaffold."

" True !" murmured Thérésine.   " If you are discovered, you are lost; you do not know how bad the
country has become.   How had you ever the courage to come here ? "

" I know it was wrong for me to come here, since
by doing so I expose you all to danger.   I should
have considered that the fatal fever which is consum-
ing France must have reached my dear country by
this time.   But as soon as my presence was useless
in Paris after the death of our beloved King and his
royal consort, I left there to join the army of the
coalition.   In order to avoid pursuit, I was obliged
to take the longest way, that is to say, through Provence.   So when I got as far as Saint-Gilles through
the mountains, I could not resist the temptation of
coming here to see you, to tell you that I am still
alive.   Besides, before I get killed, or at least before
I am expatriated for long years, I wanted to hunt
once more upon the Valcarès.   However, do not be
afraid.   I only ask you to give me shelter for one
night, and—"

" Give *you* shelter, Monsieur le Chevalier !" interrupted Bernard, impetuously—" we who are on your
lands and in your house, where you have given us
shelter? It is for your safety alone that we tremble,

even were there danger for the rest of us. Thank
God, no one suspects your presence in the country; the patriots never think of making a domiciliary
visit here, and, in any case, it would be easy to
conceal you. The domain is large, and thanks to
Marius, who has caused the fish and game laws to be
respected more strictly than your noble father ever
did in his lifetime, or than you will ever do, no
poachers dare approach the house. I do not believe there is a person on the estate capable of treachery; but there are some who might be indiscreet.
I will keep them out of the way when it is necessary.
Remain here as long as possible. During the day
you will stay with us, unless our society is wearisome
to you; or spend your time reading or writing in the
castle, for you cannot go out while it is light. But
at night you can hunt or fish from vespers till matins.
The mist is dangerous to the health, but has its own
use."

"Thanks, my brave comrade, thanks," said the
officer, warmly; "it is only what I would have expected from your devotion. I know you all well
enough to feel that I can depend upon any of you
as upon myself; but I made up my mind before I
came not to impose upon this fidelity. I can only
remain here twenty-four hours; other fugitives like
myself, implicated, as I am, in the unsuccessful plot
which was organized to save the Queen and only
succeeded in sending several of those concerned in

it to the gallows, will await me to-morrow evening on the seashore. The master of a vessel, the Grau-du-Roi, not for money, but out of generosity, will take us on board his ship. I promised to bring my comrades the result of our shooting excursion, which I will take in remembrance of your generous hospitality. I depend upon you, Marius, to row me across the Valcarès to a spot which I will indicate. There we will part, perhaps forever, but at least with the certainty that we are all living, and are friends in adversity as in prosperity, when far apart as when together."

Old Bernard was moved to tears. He would have given half his life to keep Frederic with them, but he knew the danger to which his young master would inevitably be exposed by remaining longer in France; so he answered in a trembling voice:

"I dare not say that it was wrong for you to come here; but since you have a chance of escape, take it. To-morrow night, Marius and I will accompany you to the seashore. To-morrow morning, at dawn, we will go to shoot upon the Valcarès; the ducks are not very numerous yet, but we will certainly bring down some of them, and also some other game. We will breakfast upon one of the islands, whither Thérésine can bring us some partridges which have been hanging a day or two in the larder. I hope it will not be our last hunting expedition together, though I am old; but if you do not find me here, on your return, Thérésine and Marius will receive you."

"You will be here too, my old friend," cried Frederic. "Believe me, the Revolution will not last much longer; we shall soon restore order with the army of the coalition. But away with such gloomy thoughts! Let us talk of the good old times, and of our pleasant day to-morrow. Marius, I trust to you to make all the preparations; and Thérésine, if your larder is as well stocked as Bernard hints, give me something to eat, for I am half dead with hunger and thirst."

"Fortunately, I put aside some bottles of that good Provençal wine which you used to like so much," said Bernard. "Marius, you know where it is; bring it out. What remains we will take with us in the boat."

They were soon seated round the table, where the outlaw drank toasts to his friends and to the speedy arrival of the princes, and recovered some of his old gayety and good spirits as he talked shooting and fishing with his foster-father.

The night was far advanced, when Bernard, fearing that the Chevalier would be too much fatigued, suggested that it was time to retire.

"Who will wake me?" said the young man as he went up to his old room, "for I warn you that I will sleep like a top. Will you, Marius?"

"With pleasure, Monsieur le Chevalier," said the overseer, who was quite restored to good humor.

" At what hour do you wish to start ? "

" At five o'clock. "

" That is rather too early; the mist is thick in the morning, and I advise you to wait till six. "

" Till six, then, but not later. "

" At six precisely. Sound sleep to you, Monsieur Frederic. "

" Thanks. Do not forget the guns; mine must be rusty. "

" Oh, no! " cried Bernard, " I have kept it in order myself, and I assure you it will not hang fire. "

With this they separated for the night, and an hour later all was in darkness.

" I will sleep to-night in the hay-loft," said Marius to his wife, " for I must get up very early to mend the boat. I do not want to disturb the poor Chevalier, who must be worn out. So go to bed and sleep, and do not be anxious about me. "

Thérésine made no objection, closed and bolted the door, and put out the light, but she did not sleep. Very soon after she fancied she heard a slight noise in the yard; she jumped up, peeped out through a crack in the shutter, and saw her husband in the act of bringing a horse from the stable, with its hoofs wrapped in straw. The horse was saddled and bridled. Marius led him out carefully, closed the gate after him, and in a moment more Thérésine heard the sound of a horse galloping. Where could her husband be going so stealthily ? A terrible suspicion

crossed her mind, and she at first thought of com-
municating it to her father, but on reflection she re-
frained. She did not, however, go back to bed.

"There will be time enough," thought she; and
having assured herself that the guns and the oars
were in their place, she waited in an agony of suspense for daylight. About four in the morning, the
gate of the court opened again. Thérésine saw Marius, on foot this time, gliding softly into the stable.
Over his shoulder was the harness of his horse, which
he had probably set at liberty to avert suspicion.
Half an hour later Bernard came into the kitchen; the
coffee was already made, the guns on the table. In
the chimney-corner sat Thérésine, plucking partridges.
He reproached her gently for being up so early.

"I could not sleep," said she.

"Neither could I," he answered. "The thought
of to-day's sport kept me awake."

"The weather is splendid; there will be no mist
this morning," she continued. "You had better
start at five o'clock."

"It would be better, but the Chevalier would not
be ready."

"What makes you think that, old friend?" said
Frederic himself, slapping him on the shoulder.
"Let us take our coffee and be off."

"Who woke you so very early, Monsieur Frederic?"

"Thérésine, of course. Why, what time is it?"

"Five at latest."

"What did you do that for?" said the old man, somewhat crossly, to Thérésine.

"It is such a fine morning," she answered.

"And here we are almost ready. But we shall have to wait for Marius," continued Bernard.

"I will call him," said Thérésine.

Trembling with emotion, she knocked at the stable-door.

"Who's there?" inquired a sleepy voice.

"Get up; they are waiting for you."

"How stupid! It is only five, and we do not start till half-past six," growled the voice.

"I tell you they are waiting."

"In the devil's name, give me time to get on my clothes."

Thérésine returned to the house and, having served the coffee, went and took the glass which had been left in Madame's room. As far off as she could see in the plain there were only cattle and a few guard-ians; she came down somewhat reassured. Marius had not yet appeared; he was long in dressing.

"Do you think we are going to shoot with bullets?" cried Bernard. "It was well I noticed your mistake. Look at that pouch!"

"Take them with you, father, I implore you," she said in a supplicating tone.

"I think you are crazy."

"No, but you might meet with some mischance

in going out, and I warn you that I have loaded your guns with balls. Once upon the river, you can discharge them if you like."

" Let me alone. Do you think that—"

" My dear Bernard," interrupted Frederic, " Thérésine thought she was doing for the best, and a ball more or less does not make much difference."

" Above all things, do not tell Marius; he would scold me," said Thérésine.

Just then Marius entered. He was in very bad humor at having been awakened so early, and did not want to start till the appointed hour. He suddenly noticed a pair of oars standing against the door.

" Who put those oars there ? " he asked.

" I did," said Thérésine.

" To the devil with women, who are always meddling in what does not concern them! That pair are no good."

And he would have removed them.

" Ah! those are my old oars," said Frederic, " the ones I used to prefer; it was a woman's thought. Thanks, Thérésine. Leave them, Marius; I will use them."

Thérésine left the room on some pretence, and went upstairs again. She had observed some stains of fresh mud on her husband's trousers, and she therefore knew that he must have crossed the Sansouire, which was the shortest way to Arles. She strained her eyes in the direction of the town.

Downstairs, in the kitchen, the men were drinking
their coffee. Bernard was grumbling; his son-in-law
seemed to have so many things to do, and had not
yet finished his preparations when the clock struck
six.

Thérésine suddenly rushed in, pale as death.

"Marius," said she, "go and look out at the gate;
"it seems to me that there are men coming hither
from Arles."

"I really believe that woman is determined to
drive us out of our senses," said Marius, stamping
on the ground in a rage, and with a fearful oath he
shrugged his shoulders and went out.

"Quick! quick! Take your oars and your guns,
and fly to the boat. The Blues are coming," cried
Thérésine. "I saw them; you are betrayed!"

"Betrayed? by whom?" cried Bernard.

"By him," she said, pointing after her husband.
"Last night he went and denounced the Chevalier."

"Curses on him!" cried Bernard. "Are you
sure?"

"No, but I am sure that the horsemen coming
here are the Blues. There is still time to reach the
boat; once on the water, they cannot harm you.
But fly, in the name of Heaven!"

Bernard snatched up the oars and his carabine.

"Come," said he, "Monsieur Frederic, come!"

"I will go alone. I forbid you to accompany
me, my brave friend," said the Chevalier.

"And I command you to follow me," said the old man, opening the door.

But Marius had closed the courtyard gate from without, to prevent their escape.

"This way! this way!" cried Thérésine, half-crazed with grief. "Go by the garden; the boat is there. "Take this axe, cut the moorings, and row for your lives."

All three rushed into the garden.

"Farewell, Thérésine. May Heaven reward you!" cried the outlaw, grasping the hand of the weeping woman. And leaping over the hedge, the two men rushed towards the boat.

So busy was he making signals for the Blues to hasten, that the traitor never perceived the fugitives till they had just cut the cord which secured the vessel. Then, in his mad fury, he threw off the mask.

"This way," he cried to the republicans, "this way! Fire upon those brigands!"

The horsemen came up at full gallop.

"Row for your life, Monsieur Frederic!" cried Bernard, pushing the boat off.

"Fire upon the one rowing, fire!" cried Marius, foaming with rage; and seeing that the Blues were only wasting their useless balls, he snatched a carabine from the hand of a soldier, knelt down to take surer aim, and fired. The boat gave a sudden lurch.

" For all the saints, row straight ! " roared Bernard
to Frederic.

" He has revenged my lucky shot at the partridges,"
murmured Frederic, letting go the oars and putting
one hand to a wound in his breast, while he held out
the other, all covered with blood, to his old friend.

" Monsieur le Chevalier," muttered the old man,
his face darkening with a terrible look, "do not die
for a moment."

Marius saw the fatal weapon directed against himself.   He knew that Bernard's aim was certain, and
made an effort to escape.   Bernard fired; the traitor
did not fall, though he trembled violently, and threw
up his arms with a despairing gesture.

" Be accursed, wretch ! " cried Bernard, " be accursed, murderer of your brother ! "

Standing up in the boat, his own breast a target
for the republicans, Bernard took aim again.   His
ball struck Marius in the forehead.   The wretch fell,
a shapeless mass, his face in the mud, writhed an
instant like a serpent, and was still.   Then the old
man forgot everything but his hapless master, and
knelt beside him, kissing the wound by which that
noble soul was going out, and watering his corpse
with tears.   Beside the Chevalier lay his musket,
still loaded with two balls.   Bernard never even
thought of using it, but took the oars, and, crippled
with wounds as he was, rowed on and on, until his
strength failed.   The frail canoe, riddled with balls,

was beginning to fill. Knowing that it must soon sink, Bernard bent the knee in a last prayer. Death - surprised him thus; his head had fallen on the breast of his foster-son, while the canoe, sinking gradually, disappeared at last, under the blue winding-sheet formed by the deep waters of the Valcarès, on the spot since called " the Grave of the Noble."

For many years after this tragic episode, pilgrims coming to les Saintes-Maries saw at the cemetery-gate a woman, still young and clothed in rags, who came every evening to sit beside a grave, singing softly to herself:

> " O Magali, ma tant amado,
> Mete la teste au fenestroun!
> Escouto un pau aquesto aubado
> De tambourin e de viouloun."

When she had got that far she stopped, and seemed to listen breathlessly. Alas! the voice of the Chevalier would never more take up the refrain:

> " Ei plen d'estello, aperamount!
> L'auro es toumbado."

Having listened vainly for the voice that could not come from the farther shore, she arose sorrowfully, and went to kneel on the steps of the church, where she, weeping, prayed for the souls of the departed. One year they missed her, and the poor maniac was found lifeless on the banks of the Valcarès. It was Thérésine, holding a rose in her hand, and there was a smile upon her lips.

PRINTED BY BENZIGER BROTHERS, NEW YORK.

STANDARD CATHOLIC BOOKS

PUBLISHED BY

BENZIGER BROTHERS

CINCINNATI: NEW YORK: CHICAGO:
343 MAIN ST.   J6-38 BARCLAY ST. 214-216 W. MONROE ST.

Books not marked *net* will be sent postpaid on receipt of advertised price.
Books marked *net* are such where ten per cent must be added for postage.
Thus a book advertised as *net*, $1.00, will be sent postpaid on receipt of $1.10.

Complete descriptive catalogue sent free on application.

INSTRUCTION, DOCTRINE, APOLOGETICS, CONTROVERSY, DE-
VOTION, MEDITATION, THEOLOGY, LITURGY, HOLY SCRIPTURE,
BIBLE, SERMONS, PHILOSOPHY, SCIENCE, HISTORY, BIOGRAPHY

ABANDONMENT; or, Absolute Surrender of Self to Divine Providence. CAUSSADE, S.J.	net, 0 50
ADORATION OF THE BLESSED SACRAMENT. TESNIÈRE.	0 50
ANECDOTES AND EXAMPLES ILLUSTRATING THE CATHOLIC CATECHISM. SPIRAGO.	net, 1 50
ANGELS OF THE SANCTUARY. For Altar Boys. MUSSER.	net, 0 15
AUTOBIOGRAPHY OF ST. IGNATIUS. O'CONOR, S.J.	net, 1 25
BEGINNINGS OF CHRISTIANITY, THE. A history of conditions of Christian life in the first three centuries of our era. SHAHAN.	net, 2 00
BENEDICENDA; or, Rites and Ceremonies to be Observed in some of the Principal Functions of the Roman Pontifical and Roman Ritual. SCHULTE.	net, 1 50
BIBLE, THE HOLY. Large type, handy size. Cloth, 1.00; finer bindings, 1.50—4.00; India paper edition,	3 00—5 00
BONOMELLI, RT. REV. J. HOMILIES ON THE EPISTLES AND GOSPELS. 4 vols.	net, 5 00
—HOMILIES ON THE COMMON OF SAINTS. 2 vols.	net, 2 50
—THE CHRISTIAN MYSTERIES; or, Discourses for all the Great Feasts except Those of the Blessed Virgin. 4 vols.	net, 5 00
BOOK OF THE PROFESSED. Vols. I, II, III. Each,	net, 0 75
BOY-SAVER'S GUIDE. Society Work for Lads in Their Teens. QUIN, S.J.	net, 1 35
CASES OF CONSCIENCE for English-speaking Countries. SLATER, S.J. 2 vols.	net, 3 50
CATECHISM EXPLAINED. SPIRAGO-CLARKE.	net, 2 50
CATHOLIC BELIEF. FAÀ DI BRUNO. Paper, net, 0.10; Cloth,	net, 0 35
CATHOLIC CEREMONIES. DURAND. Ill. Paper, 0.20; Cloth,	0 50
CATHOLIC HOME ANNUAL. Calendar, Stories, etc. Ill.	0 25
CATHOLIC PRACTICE AT CHURCH AND AT HOME. KLAUDER. Paper, 0.25; Cloth,	0 60
CATHOLIC WORSHIP. BRENNAN. Paper, *list price*, 0.15; Cloth, *list price*,	0 22
CATHOLIC'S READY ANSWER, THE. REV. M. P. HILL, S.J.	net, 2 00
CEREMONIAL FOR ALTAR BOYS. BRITT.	net, 0 35
CHILD PREPARED FOR FIRST COMMUNION, THE. ZULUETA, S.J.	0 05
CHRISTIAN APOLOGETICS. A Defense of the Catholic Faith. DEVIVIER-MESSMER.	net, 2 00
CHRISTIAN EDUCATION. O'CONNELL.	net, 0 60
CHRISTIAN FATHER, THE. Instructions. CRAMER. Paper, 0.15; Cloth,	0 35

GROWTH AND DEVELOPMENT OF THE CATHOLIC
   SCHOOL SYSTEM IN THE UNITED STATES. Burns.   *net,* 1 75
GUIDE FOR SACRISTANS.   *net,* 0 85
HANDBOOK OF THE CHRISTIAN RELIGION. Wilmers, S.J. *net,* 1 50
HARMONY OF THE RELIGIOUS LIFE. Heuser.   *net,* 1 25
HELPS TO A SPIRITUAL LIFE. Schneider.   0 50
HIDDEN TREASURE; or, The Value and Excellence of Holy
   Mass. Blessed Leonard. Paper, 0.15; Cloth,   0 35
HISTORY OF THE CATHOLIC CHURCH. Alzog. 3 vols. *net,* 8 00
HISTORY OF THE CATHOLIC CHURCH. Businger-Bren-
  nan. 8vo.   2 00
HISTORY OF THE CATHOLIC CHURCH. Brueck. 2 vols. *net,* 3 00
HISTORY OF ECONOMICS. Dewe.   *net,* 1 50
HISTORY OF THE MASS. O'Brien.   *net,* 1 25
HISTORY OF THE PROTESTANT REFORMATION. Cobbett. 0 50
HOLY EUCHARIST, THE. Liguori.   *net,* 1 50
HOLY HOUR, THE. Keiley.   0 05
HOLY MASS, THE. Liguori.   *net,* 1 50
HOLY VIATICUM OF LIFE AS OF DEATH, THE. A pro-
  vision for the journey of life as well as of death. Dever.
  Paper, 0.25; Cloth.   0.60
HOLY WEEK, COMPLETE OFFICE OF. Cheap Edition,
  flexible cloth, *net,* 0.20; Cloth,   *net,* 0 30
HOW TO COMFORT THE SICK. Krebs.   0 50
HOW TO MAKE THE MISSION.   0 10
INCARNATION, BIRTH, AND INFANCY OF CHRIST,
  Liguori.   *net,* 1 50
INDEX TO LIGUORI'S WORKS.   *net,* 0 10
IN HEAVEN WE KNOW OUR OWN. For those who have lost
  dear ones by death. Blot, S.J.   *net,* 0 60
INSTRUCTIONS FOR FIRST COMMUNICANTS. Schmitt. *net,* 0 60
INSTRUCTIONS ON THE COMMANDMENTS AND SACRA-
  MENTS. Liguori. Paper, 0.15; Cloth.   0 35
INSTRUCTIONS ON MARRIAGE, POPULAR. Girardey.
  Paper, 0.15; Cloth,   0.35
INTERIOR OF JESUS AND MARY. Grou, S.J. 2 vols. *net,* 2 00
JESUS LIVING IN THE PRIEST. Millet-Byrne.   *net,* 2 00
LADY, A. Manners and Social Usages. Bugg.   0 50
LAWS OF THE KING. Talks on the Commandments for Chil-
  dren.   0 60
LESSONS OF THE SAVIOUR. Christ's Miracles Described for
  Children.   0 60
LETTERS OF ST. ALPHONSUS LIGUORI. 5 vols. Each. *net,* 1 50
LIFE OF BL. MARGARET MARY ALACOQUE. Bougaud. 0 50
LIFE OF POPE PIUS X.   2 00
LIFE OF ST. CATHERINE OF SIENNA. Aymé.   1 00
LIFE OF THE BLESSED VIRGIN. Rohner-Brennan.   0 50
LIFE OF CHRIST AND OF HIS BLESSED MOTHER.
  Businger-Brennan. Profusely illustrated.   *net,* 10 00
LIFE OF CHRIST. Cochem-Hammer.   0 50
LIFE OF SISTER ANNE KATHARINE EMMERICH.
  McGowan.   *net,* 1 75
LIFE OF ST. TERESA, POPULAR. Rev. M. Joseph.   0 50
LIFE OF VEN. CRESCENTIA HÖSS.   *net,* 1 25
LIGUORI. COMPLETE WORKS. Vols. I-XXII. Each, *net,* 1 50
LITTLE COMMUNICANTS' PRAYER-BOOK. Sloan.   0 20
LITTLE MANUAL OF ST. RITA. McGrath.   0 50
LITTLE MASS BOOK. Lynch.   0 05
LIVES OF THE SAINTS. Adapted from Alban Butler.   0 50
LIVES OF THE SAINTS FOR CHILDREN. Berthold.   0 60
LIVES OF THE SAINTS, PICTORIAL. Shea. Illustrated. 3 00
LIVES OF THE SAINTS, SHORT. Donnelly.   0 60
LIVES OF THE SAINTS, LITTLE PICTORIAL. Illustrated. 1 25
LOURDES. Its Inhabitants, Its Pilgrims and Miracles. Clarke, S.J. 0 50
MANUAL OF CATHOLIC HYMNS. Dieringer-Pierron. Edi-
  tion with melody and words, *list price,* 0.42; Edition for
  the organist,   *net,* 3 00
MANUAL OF HOMILETICS AND CATECHETICS. Schuech. *net,* 1 25
MANUAL OF MORAL THEOLOGY. Slater, S.J. Vols. I
  and II. Each,   *net,* 2 75

3

4

PATRON SAINTS FOR CATHOLIC YOUTH. Illustrated.
Vols. I, II, III. MANNIX. Each.   0 60
PEARLS FROM FABER. Selections from His Works BRUNOWE.   0 35
POLITICAL AND MORAL ESSAYS. RICKABY, S.J.   net, 1 75
PRAXIS SYNODALIS.   net, 0 75
PREACHING. LIGUORI.   net, 1 50
PREPARATION FOR DEATH. LIGUORI.   net, 1 50
PRINCIPLES, ORIGIN, AND ESTABLISHMENT OF THE
    CATHOLIC SCHOOL SYSTEM IN THE U. S. BURNS.   net, 1 75
PRIVATE RETREAT FOR RELIGIOUS. GEIERMANN,
    C.SS.R.   net, 1 50
PULPIT SKETCHES. Outlines of Sermons. LAMBERT.   net, 1 25
QUESTIONS OF MORAL THEOLOGY. REV. THOMAS
    SLATER, S.J.   net, 2 00
RAMBLES IN CATHOLIC LANDS. REV. MICHAEL BARRETT,
    O.S.B.   net, 2 00
REASONABLENESS OF CATHOLIC CEREMONIES AND
    PRACTICES. BURKE. Paper, 0.15; Cloth,   0 35
RELIGIOUS STATE, THE. LIGUORI.   net, 0 50
RETREATS FOR SISTERS, TWO. WIRTH.   net, 1 00
RITUALE COMPENDIOSUM. Sacristy Ritual.   net, 0 90
ROMA. Ancient, Subterranean, and Modern Rome in Word and
    Picture. By REV. ALBERT KUHN, O.S.B., D.D. Preface by
    CARDINAL GIBBONS. 18 bi-monthly parts, each 0.35 postpaid.
    Subscription by the year, 6 parts, 2.00; complete work. 6.00.
    938 text illustrations, 40 full-page illustrations, 3 plans of
    Rome in colors. The best and most thorough production of
    its kind.
ROMAN CURIA AS IT NOW EXISTS. MARTIN, S.J.   net, 1 50
ROSARY, THE CROWN OF MARY, THE.   0 10
RULES OF LIFE FOR THE PASTOR OF SOULS. SLATER-
    RAUCH.   net, 0 75
SACRAMENTALS. The Sacramentals of the Church Explained.
    LAMBING. Paper, 0.20; Cloth,   0 50
SACRED HEART STUDIED IN THE SACRED SCRIP-
    TURES, THE. SAINTRAIN, C.SS.R.   0 50
SACRIFICE OF THE MASS WORTHILY CELEBRATED.
    CHAIGNON, S.J.   net, 1 50
SAINTS AND PLACES. AYSCOUGH. Description of Italy's
    most historic spots. 22 full-page illustrations. net, 1 50
ST. ANTHONY. ANECDOTES AND EXAMPLES. KELLER.   net, 0 75
ST. ANTHONY, THE SAINT OF THE WHOLE WORLD.
    WARD.   0 50
SAINT FRANCIS OF ASSISI: SOCIAL REFORMER.
    DUBOIS.   0 50
SCAPULAR MEDAL, THE. REV. P. GEIERMANN, C.SS.R.   0 05
SECRET OF SANCTITY. CRASSET.   0 50
SELF-KNOWLEDGE AND CHRISTIAN PERFECTION.
    HENRY. Paper, 0.25; Cloth,   0 60
SERMONS FOR CHILDREN OF MARY. CALLERIO.   net, 1 50
SERMONS FOR CHILDREN'S MASSES. FRASSINETTI.   net, 1 50
SERMONS FOR SUNDAYS. LIGUORI.   net, 1 50
SERMONS FOR THE SUNDAYS AND CHIEF FESTIVALS
    OF THE ECCLESIASTICAL YEAR. 2 vols. POTTGEISSER. net, 3 00
SERMONS FROM THE LATINS. BAXTER.   net, 2 00
SERMONS, FUNERAL. WIRTH. Vols. I and II. Each,   net, 1 00
SERMONS, NEW AND OLD. WIRTH. 8 vols. Each,   net, 2 00
SERMONS ON THE BLESSED SACRAMENT. SCHEURER-
    LASANCE.   net, 1 50
SERMONS ON THE CATECHISM, POPULAR. BAMBERG-
    THURSTON, S.J. 3 vols. Each,   net, 1 50
SERMONS ON THE DEVOTION TO THE SACRED HEART,
    Six. BIERBAUM.   net, 0 75
SERMONS, SHORT, FOR LOW MASSES. SCHOUPPE.   net, 1 25
SERMONS, SHORT. HUNOLT. 5 vols. (WIRTH.) Each,   net, 2 00
SHORT CONFERENCES ON THE SACRED HEART. BRINK-
    MEYER,   0 50
SHORT COURSE IN CATHOLIC DOCTRINE. For Non-
    Catholics Intending Marriage with Catholics.   0 10
SHORT HISTORY OF MORAL THEOLOGY. SLATER, S.J.   net, 0 50
SHORT MEDITATIONS FOR EVERY DAY. LASAUSSE.   0 50

5

SOCIALISM AND CHRISTIANITY. Stang. *net*, 1 00
SOCIALISM: ITS THEORETICAL BASIS AND PRACTICAL
APPLICATION. Cathrein, S.J. *net*, 1 50
SOCIALISM, MORALITY OF MODERN. Ming, S.J. *net*, 1 50
SOCIALISM, CHARACTERISTICS AND RELIGION OF.
Ming, S.J. *net*, 1 50
SPECIAL INTRODUCTION TO THE STUDY OF THE OLD
TESTAMENT. Part I. Gigot. *net*, 1 50
SPECIAL INTRODUCTION TO THE STUDY OF THE OLD
TESTAMENT. Part II. Gigot. *net*, 2 00
SPIRAGO'S METHOD OF CHRISTIAN DOCTRINE. Mess-
mer. *net*, 1 50
SPIRITUAL CONSIDERATIONS. Buckler, O.P. 0 50
SPIRITUAL DESPONDENCY AND TEMPTATIONS.
Michel, S.J. *net*, 1 25
SPIRITUAL EXERCISES FOR A TEN DAYS' RETREAT.
Smetana, C.SS.R. *net*, 0 75
SPIRITUAL PEPPER AND SALT. Stang. Paper, 0.25;
Cloth, 0 60
SPIRIT OF SACRIFICE AND THE LIFE OF SACRIFICE
IN THE RELIGIOUS STATE. Giraud-Thurston. *net*, 2 00
SPOILING THE DIVINE FEAST. Zulueta. 0 05
STORIES FOR FIRST COMMUNICANTS. Keller. *net*, 0 50
STORY OF THE DIVINE CHILD. Lings. 0 60
SUNDAY-SCHOOL DIRECTOR'S GUIDE. Sloan. *net*, 0 50
SUNDAY-SCHOOL TEACHER'S GUIDE. Sloan. 0 50
SURE WAY TO A HAPPY MARRIAGE. Paper, 0.15; Cloth, 0 35
TALKS WITH THE LITTLE ONES ABOUT THE APOS-
TLES' CREED. 0 60
THEORY AND PRACTICE OF THE CONFESSIONAL.
Schieler-Heuser. *net*, 3 50
THOUGHTS AND AFFECTIONS ON THE PASSION OF
JESUS CHRIST FOR EVERY DAY IN THE YEAR.
Bergamo. *net*, 2 00
THOUGHTS ON THE RELIGIOUS LIFE. Lasance. *net*, 1 50
TRAINING OF CHILDREN. Madame Cecilia. Paper, 0.25; Cloth, 0 60
TRUE POLITENESS, LETTERS ON. Demore. *net*, 0 75
TRUE SPOUSE OF CHRIST. Liguori. 0 50
TRUE SPOUSE OF CHRIST. Vols. I and II. Liguori. Each, *net*, 1 50
VENERATION OF THE BLESSED VIRGIN. Rohner-Bren-
nan. 0 50
VICTORIES OF THE MARTYRS. Liguori. *net*, 1 50
VIGIL HOUR. Ryan, S.J. 0 05
VISIT TO EUROPE AND THE HOLY LAND. Fairbanks. 1 50
VOCATION. Van Tricht-Conniff. Paper, 0 05
VOCATIONS EXPLAINED. 0 10
WAY OF THE CROSS. Paper, 0 05
WAY OF THE CROSS. Illustrated. Eucharistic Method. 0 10
WAY OF THE CROSS. Illustrated. Method of St. Francis
Assisi. 0 10
WAY OF THE CROSS. Illustrated. Method of Jesuit Father. 0 10
WAY OF THE CROSS. Illustrated. Method of St. Alphon-
sus Liguori. 0 10
WAY OF SALVATION AND OF PERFECTION. Meditations.
Liguori. *net*, 1 50
WAY OF INTERIOR PEACE. De Lehen. *net*, 1 50
WHAT CATHOLICS HAVE DONE FOR SCIENCE. Bren-
nan. *net*, 1 25
WHAT THE CHURCH TEACHES. Drury. Paper, 0.25;
Cloth, 0 60
WITH CHRIST, MY FRIEND. Sloan. *net*, 0 75

NOVELS, POETRY, ETC.

AGATHA'S HARD SAYING. Rosa Mulholland. 0 50
BACK TO THE WORLD. Champol. *net*, 1 35
BALLADS OF CHILDHOOD. By Rev. Michael Earls, S.J. *net*, 1 00
BLACK BROTHERHOOD, THE. Garrold, S.J. *net*, 1 35
BOND AND FREE. Connor. 0 50
"BUT THY LOVE AND THY GRACE." Finn, S.J. 1 00
BY THE BLUE RIVER. Isabel C. Clarke. .. *net*, 1 35

ROUND THE WORLD SERIES. Vol. I.	⎫	1 00
ROUND THE WORLD SERIES. Vol. II.		1 00
ROUND THE WORLD SERIES. Vol. III.	A series of inter-	1 00
ROUND THE WORLD SERIES. Vol. IV.	esting articles on a	1 00
ROUND THE WORLD SERIES. Vol. V.	great variety of sub-	1 00
ROUND THE WORLD SERIES. Vol. VI.	jects of much educa-	1 00
ROUND THE WORLD SERIES. Vol. VII.	tional value. Pro-	1 00
ROUND THE WORLD SERIES. Vol. VIII.	fusely illustrated.	1 00
ROUND THE WORLD SERIES. Vol. IX.		1 00
ROUND THE WORLD SERIES. Vol. X.	⎭	1 00

 RULER OF THE KINGDOM, THE. KEON. 1 25
SECRET CITADEL, THE. ISABEL C. CLARKE. *net,* 1 35
SECRET OF THE GREEN VASE, THE. COOKE. 0 50
SENIOR LIEUTENANT'S WAGER, THE, AND OTHER
   STORIES. 0 60
SHADOW OF EVERSLEIGH, THE. LANSDOWNE. 0 50
SHIELD OF SILENCE. M. E. HENRY-RUFFIN. *net,* 1 35
SO AS BY FIRE. CONNOR. 0 50
SOGGARTH AROON. GUINAN. 1 25
SON OF SIRO, THE. COPUS. *net,* 1 35
STORY OF CECILIA, THE. HINKSON. 1 25
STUORE. EARLS. 1 00
TEMPEST OF THE HEART, THE. GRAY. 0 50
TEST OF COURAGE, THE. ROSS. 0 50
THAT MAN'S DAUGHTER. ROSS. 1 25
THEIR CHOICE. SKINNER. 0 50
THROUGH THE DESERT. SIENKIEWICZ. *net,* 1 35
TRAIL OF THE DRAGON, THE, AND OTHER STORIES. 0 50
TRAINING OF SILAS. DEVINE. S.J. 1 25
TRUE STORY OF MASTER GERARD, THE. SADLIER. 1 25
TURN OF THE TIDE, THE. GRAY. 0 50
UNBIDDEN GUEST, THE. COOKE. 0 50
UNRAVELING OF A TANGLE, THE. TAGGART. 1 25
UP IN ARDMUIRLAND. BARRETT. *net,* 1 25
VOCATION OF EDWARD CONWAY, THE. EGAN. 1 25
WARGRAVE TRUST, THE. REID. 1 25
WAY THAT LED BEYOND, THE. HARRISON. 1 25
WEDDING BELLS OF GLENDALOUGH, THE. EARLS. *net,* 1 35
WHEN LOVE IS STRONG. KEON. 1 25
WOMAN OF FORTUNE. CHRISTIAN REID. 1 25

JUVENILES

ALTHEA. NIRDLINGER. 0 50
ADVENTURE WITH THE APACHES, AN. FERRY. 0 35
AS GOLD IN THE FURNACE. COPUS, S.J. 0 85
AS TRUE AS GOLD. MANNIX. 0 35
BELL FOUNDRY, THE. SCHACHING. 0 35
BERKLEYS, THE. WIGHT. 0 35
BEST FOOT FORWARD, THE. FINN, S.J. 0 85
BETWEEN FRIENDS. AUMERLE. 0 50
BISTOURI. MELANDRI. 0 35
BLISSYLVANIA POST-OFFICE, THE. TAGGART. 0 35
BOB O'LINK. WAGGERMAN. 0 35
BROWNIE AND I. AUMERLE. 0 50
BUNT AND BILL. C. MULHOLLAND. 0 35
BY BRANSCOME RIVER. TAGGART. 0 35
CAMP BY COPPER RIVER, THE. SPALDING, S.J. 0 85
CAPTAIN TED. WAGGAMAN. 0 50
CAVE BY THE BEECH FORK, THE. SPALDING. 0 85
CHARLIE CHITTYWICK. BEARNE. 0 85
CHILDREN OF CUPA. MANNIX. 0 35
CHILDREN OF THE LOG CABIN. DELAMARE. 0 50
CLARE LORAINE. "LEE." 0 50
CLAUDE LIGHTFOOT. FINN, S.J. 0 85
COLLEGE BOY, A. YORKE. 0 85
CUPA REVISITED. MANNIX. 0 35
DADDY DAN. WAGGAMAN. 0 35
DEAR FRIENDS. NIRDLINGER. 0 60
DIMPLING'S SUCCESS. C. MULHOLLAND. 0 35

9

QUEEN'S PROMISE, THE. Waggaman.   0 50
RACE FOR COPPER ISLAND, THE. Spalding, S.J.   0 85
RECRUIT TOMMY COLLINS. Bonesteel.   0 35
RIDINGDALE FLOWER SHOW. Bearne, S.J.   0 85
ROMANCE OF THE SILVER SHOON. Bearne, S.J.   0 85
SANDY JOE. Waggaman.   0 85
SEA-GULL'S ROCK, THE. Sandeau.   0 35
SEVEN LITTLE MARSHALLS, THE. Nixon-Roulet.   0 35
SHADOWS LIFTED. Copus, S.J.   0 85
SHEER PLUCK. Bearne, S.J.   0 85
SHERIFF OF THE BEECH FORK, THE. Spalding, S.J.   0 85
SHIPMATES. Waggaman.   0 50
ST. CUTHBERT'S. Copus, S.J.   0 85
STRONG-ARM OF AVALON. Waggaman.   0 85
SUGAR-CAMP AND AFTER, THE. Spalding, S.J.   0 85
SUMMER AT WOODVILLE, A. Sadlier.   0 35
TALES AND LEGENDS OF THE MIDDLE AGES. Capella.   0 75
TALISMAN, THE. Sadlier.   0 50
TAMING OF POLLY, THE. Dorsey.   0 85
THAT FOOTBALL GAME. Finn, S.J.   0 85
THAT OFFICE BOY. Finn, S.J.   0 85
THREE GIRLS AND ESPECIALLY ONE. Taggart.   0 35
TOLD IN THE TWILIGHT. Mother Salome.   0 50
TOM LOSELY: BOY. Copus, S.J.   0 85
TOM'S LUCK-POT. Waggaman.   0 35
TOM PLAYFAIR. Finn, S.J.   0 85
TOORALLADDY. Walsh.   0 35
TRANSPLANTING OF TESSIE, THE. Waggaman.   0 50
TREASURE OF NUGGET MOUNTAIN, THE. Taggart.   0 50
TWO LITTLE GIRLS. Mack.   0 35
UPS AND DOWNS OF MARJORIE. Waggaman.   0 35
VIOLIN MAKER OF MITTENWALD, THE. Schaching.   0 35
WAYWARD WINIFRED. Sadlier.   0 85
WINNETOU, THE APACHE KNIGHT. Taggart.   0 50
WITCH OF RIDINGDALE, THE. Bearne, S.J.   0 85
YOUNG COLOR GUARD, THE. Bonesteel.   0 35

BENZIGER'S STANDARD FIFTY-CENT LIBRARY FOR EVERYBODY

Novels, Juveniles and Religious Books by the best Catholic Authors. Copyright books. Substantially and attractively bound in cloth. Complete list of books in library sent on application. Each volume, $0.50.

BENZIGER'S THIRTY-FIVE-CENT JUVENILE LIBRARY

Books for young folks by the best authors. Copyright books. They are printed on good paper in large and readable type, and are neatly bound in cloth. Each book has an illustrated jacket. Complete list on request. Each volume, $0.35.

CATHOLIC LIBRARIES

Books of Religious Instruction, Novels, and Juveniles, put up in libraries of 10 volumes, at $5.00. Payable on the Easy Payment Plan of $1.00 a month. List of libraries sent on application.

SCHOOL-BOOKS

Catechisms, Readers (The Catholic National Readers, The New Century Readers), Charts, Spellers, Grammars, Bible History, United States Histories, Benziger's Advanced Geography, Benziger's Elementary Geography, Graded Arithmetics, Three-Book Series of Arithmetics, Hymnbooks, etc., etc. Complete list sent on application.

PRAYER-BOOKS

Complete illustrated catalogue will be sent on application.

Sizes of books in inches: 48mo, about 3¼ x 2¼; large 48mo, about 4 x 2⅞; small 32mo, about 4⅛ x 3; 32mo, about 4¾ x 3¼; oblong 32mo, about 5¼ x 3½; 24mo, about 5½ x 3¾; oblong 24mo, about 5½ x 3½; 16mo, about 6¼ x 4½; small 12mo, 7 x 5.

FATHER LASANCE'S PRAYER-BOOKS

	Imitation Leather, Red Edges.	Leather, Gilt Edges.
MISSAL, THE NEW. In English. For Every Day in the Year. With Introduction, Notes, and a Book of Prayer.	1 50	2 00—5 00
MY PRAYER-BOOK: HAPPINESS IN GOODNESS. Reflections, Counsels, Prayers and Devotions. 16mo.	1 25	1 75—2 50
MY PRAYER-BOOK. India Paper edition. 16mo.		2 00—4 25
MY PRAYER-BOOK. India Paper edition. With Epistles and Gospels. 16mo.		2 25—2 75
BLESSED SACRAMENT BOOK. Offers a larger and greater variety of prayers than any other book in English. Large 16mo.	1 50	2 00—4 50
WITH GOD. A Book of Prayers and Reflections. 16mo.	1 25	1 75—5 00
THE YOUNG MAN'S GUIDE. For manly boys and young men. Oblong 24mo.	0 75	1 25—2 50
THE CATHOLIC GIRL'S GUIDE. Counsels for Girls in the Ordinary Walks of Life and in Particular for the Children of Mary. Oblong 16mo.	1 25	1 75—2 50
PRAYER-BOOK FOR RELIGIOUS. A complete manual of prayers for members of all religious communities. Small 12mo. *net,*	1 50	2 50—3 50
THOUGHTS ON THE RELIGIOUS LIFE. Reflections on the General Principles of the Religious Life, on Perfect Charity. Small 12mo. *net,*	1 50	2 50
VISITS TO JESUS IN THE TABERNACLE. Hours and Half-Hours of Adoration before the Blessed Sacrament. 16mo.	1 25	1 75—2 75
MANUAL OF THE HOLY EUCHARIST. Conferences on the Blessed Sacrament and Eucharistic Devotions. Oblong 24mo.	0 75	1 25
SHORT VISITS TO THE BLESSED SACRAMENT. Oblong 32mo. Cloth.	0 15	
MASS DEVOTIONS AND READINGS ON THE MASS. Twelve methods of hearing Mass. Oblong 24mo.	0 75	1 25
THE SACRED HEART BOOK. Oblong 24mo.	0 75	1 25
LITTLE MANUAL OF ST. ANTHONY. Oblong 32mo. Cloth.	0 15	

PRAYER-BOOKS FOR GENERAL USE

	Cloth.	Leather, Gilt Edges.
ALL FOR JESUS. With Epistles and Gospels. Small 32mo.	0 30	0 60—1 90
BREAD OF LIFE, THE. A Complete Communion Book for Catholics. By Rev. F. Willam. Oblong 24mo.	0 75	1 25
COME, LET US ADORE. A Eucharistic Manual. By Rev. B. Hammer, O.F.M. Small 32mo.	0 75	1 25
DEVOTIONS AND PRAYERS BY ST. ALPHONSUS LIGUORI. A Complete Manual of Pious Exercises for Every Day, Every Week, and Every Month. Ward. 16mo.	1 25	1 75
DEVOTIONS AND PRAYERS FOR THE SICK-ROOM. A Book for Every Catholic Family. By Rev. J. A. Krebs, C.SS.R. 12mo.	0 50	
DOMINICAN MISSION BOOK. By a Dominican Father. 16mo.	0 75	1 50

11

	Cloth.	Leather, Gilt Edges.
FLOWERS OF PIETY. Approved Prayers for Catholics. 48mo.	0 25	0 50—3 25
FOLLOWING OF CHRIST, THE. By THOMAS À. KEMPIS. With Reflections, etc. 32mo.	0 35	0 65
FOLLOWING OF CHRIST, THE. By THOMAS À. KEMPIS. Illustrated. India Paper. Edition de Luxe. 32mo.		1 25—3 30
GARLAND OF PRAYER, THE. A dainty prayer-book. Contains Nuptial Mass. 32mo.		2 25—3 25
GOLDEN KEY TO HEAVEN. With Epistles and Gospels. Small 32mo.	0 35	0 70—1 10
HELP FOR THE POOR SOULS IN PURGATORY. By Jos. ACKERMANN. Small 32mo.	0 60	
HOLY HOUR OF ADORATION, THE. By RIGHT REV. W. STANG, D.D. Oblong 24mo.	0 60	
IMITATION OF THE SACRED HEART OF JESUS. By REV. FR. ARNOUDT, S.J. 16mo. net,	1 25	1 75
INTRODUCTION TO A DEVOUT LIFE. By ST. FRANCIS DE SALES. Small 32mo.	0 50	
KEY OF HEAVEN, THE. With Epistles and Gospels. 48mo.	0 25	0 60—1 50
LITTLE MANUAL OF ST. RITA. Prayers and Devotions. With the Story of Her Life. By REV. THOMAS S. MCGRATH.	0 50	0 75
LITTLE MASS BOOK. By RIGHT REV. MGR. J. S. M. LYNCH. Paper. 32mo.	0 10	
MANUAL OF THE HOLY NAME. 24mo.	0 50	1 10
MANUAL OF THE SACRED HEART, NEW. Oblong 24mo.	0 25	0 75—1 25
MANUAL OF ST. ANTHONY, NEW. 32mo.	0 50	
MANUAL OF ST. JOSEPH, LITTLE. By RIGHT REV. MGR. A. A. LINGS. Oblong 32mo.	0 15	
MISSION-BOOK FOR THE MARRIED. By REV. F. GIRARDEY, C.SS.R. 32mo.	0 50	1 00
MISSION-BOOK FOR THE SINGLE. By REV. F. GIRARDEY, C.SS.R. 32mo.	0 50	1 00
MISSION-BOOK OF THE REDEMPTORIST FATHERS, THE. 32mo.	0 50	1 00
MISSION REMEMBRANCE OF THE REDEMPTORIST FATHERS. By REV. P. GEIERMANN. 32mo.	0 50	1 00
OFFICE OF HOLY WEEK, THE, COMPLETE. 16mo. Flexible Cloth, net, 0.20; Cloth, net,	0 30	0 70
OUR FAVORITE DEVOTIONS. By RIGHT REV. MGR. A. A. LINGS. Oblong 24mo.	0 75	1 25
OUR FAVORITE NOVENAS. By RIGHT REV. MGR. A. A. LINGS. Oblong 24mo.	0 75	1 25
POCKET COMPANION. Approved Prayers. Oblong 48mo.	0 10	
SERAPHIC GUIDE, THE. 24mo.	0 60	0 75
VEST-POCKET GEMS OF DEVOTION. Ob. 32mo.	0 15	0 45—0 90
VEST-POCKET GEMS OF DEVOTION. India Paper Edition. With Epistles and Gospels. Oblong 32mo.	0 45	0 65—1 25
VISITS TO THE MOST HOLY SACRAMENT AND TO THE BLESSED VIRGIN MARY. By ST. ALPHONSUS LIGUORI. 32mo.	0 35	0 75

PRAYER-BOOKS WITH LARGE TYPE

	Cloth.	Leather, Gilt Edges.
KEY OF HEAVEN. With Epistles and Gospels. 24mo.	0 50	0 90—1 70
POCKET MANUAL. Epistles and Gospels. Ob. 32mo.	0 25	0 50—1 35
WAY TO HEAVEN. With Epistles and Gospels.	0 35	0 75

PRAYER-BOOKS FOR CHILDREN AND FIRST COMMUNICANTS

	Cloth.	Leather, Gilt Edges.
BREAD OF ANGELS. Instructions and Prayers Especially Suited for First Communicants. By REV. B. HAMMER, O.F.M. Large 48mo.	0 25	0 65—0 95
CHILD OF MARY, THE. Especially for the Use of First Communicants. 32mo.	0 45	0 95

12